FEVER KNIGHTS

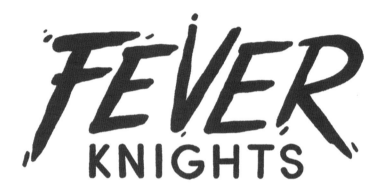

OFFICIAL FAKE
STRATEGY GUIDE

ADAM ELLIS

Andrews McMeel
PUBLISHING®

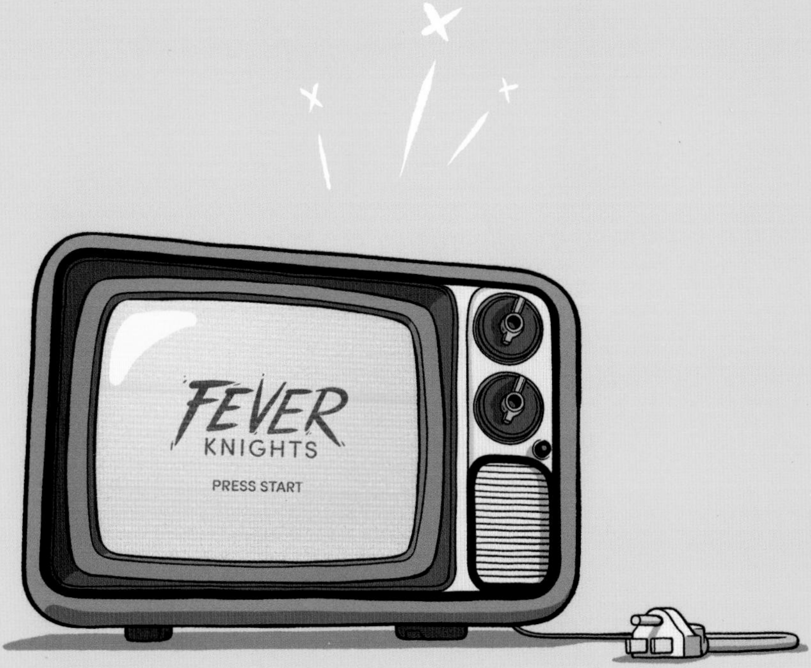
FEVER
KNIGHTS
PRESS START

LOADING GAME...

Welcome to the world of **Fever Knights**!

This book is based on the strategy guides I used to read as a kid that were often the only way for me to experience video games at all. I couldn't afford to buy games often, but my mom worked at a bookstore in the summers that had a gaming section full of guidebooks for games like *Earthbound*, *Final Fantasy*, and *Breath of Fire*. I'd go into my mom's work, grab a guide off the shelf, sit on the floor, and read the entire thing in an afternoon.

Fever Knights is inspired by my love of strategy guides, with their tightly organized glossaries of enemies, bosses, and items. Unlike traditional guides, this book is meant to be read cover to cover, with the narrative slowly unfolding chronologically as a video game would.

Now, let's go explore the island!

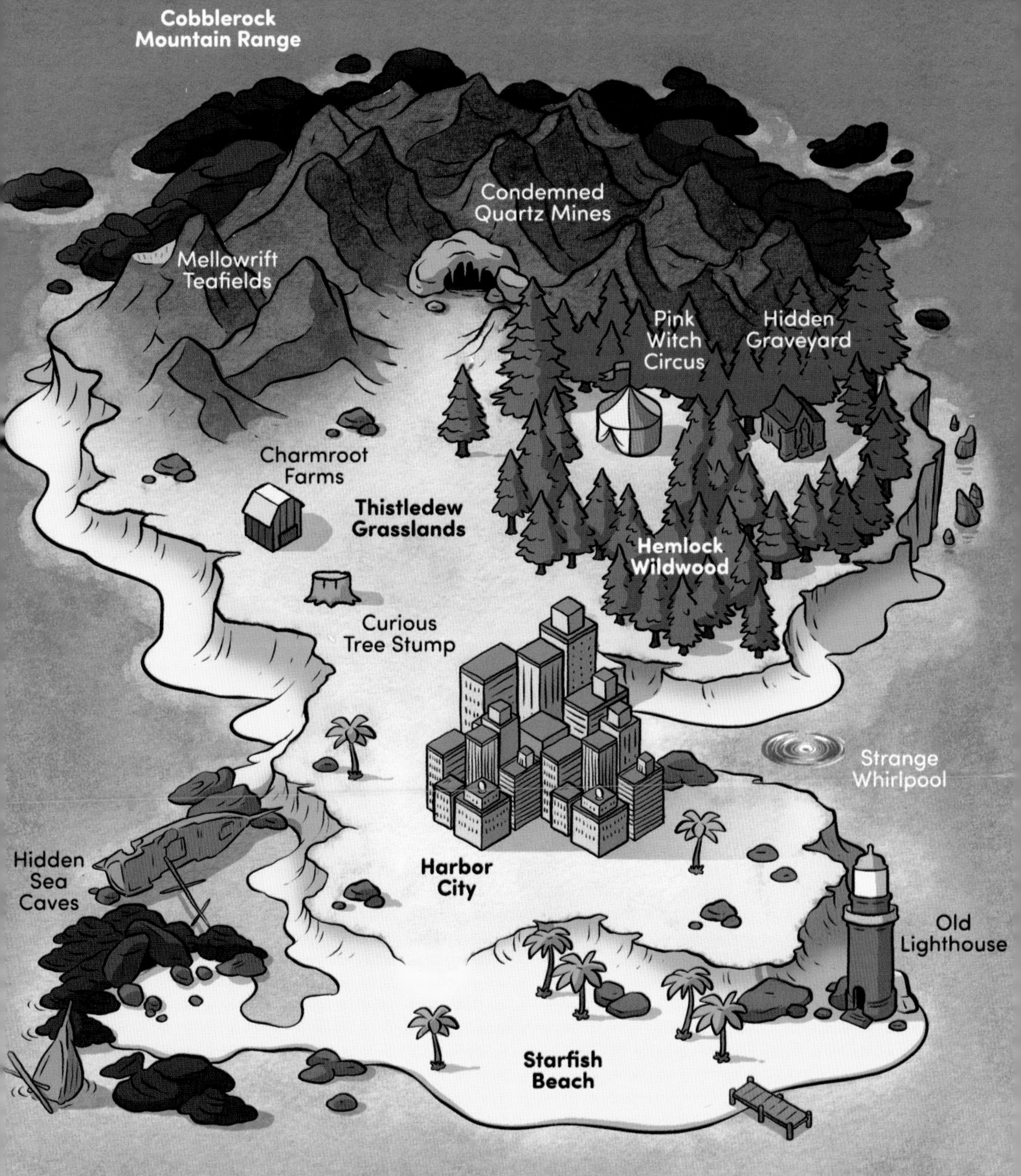
Cobblerock
Mountain Range
Condemned
Quartz Mines
Mellowrift
Teafields
Pink
Witch
Circus
Hidden
Graveyard
Charmroot
Farms
Thistledew
Grasslands
Hemlock
Wildwood
Curious
Tree Stump
Strange
Whirlpool
Hidden
Sea
Caves
Harbor
City
Old
Lighthouse
Starfish
Beach

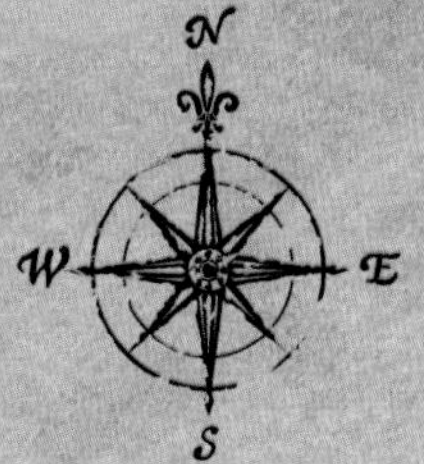
N
W
E
S

Toro Island

Southernmost Island of the Saltbrine Archipelago

FINNEUS

STATS

WEAPON: BATS

STRENGTH	●●●●●●○○○○	
DEFENSE	●●●●○○○○○○	
MAGIC	●●○○○○○○○○	

SPEED	●●●●●●●○○○	
GUTS	●●●●●●●●○○	
LUCK	●○○○○○○○○○	

AFFINITIES

FIRE	WATER	LIGHTNING	WIND	DEBUFFS	SHADOW	LIGHT
C-	C+	C-	D+	D	F	A+

BIO

Finneus had plans to surf every day of summer vacation until the big accident at **Starfish Beach** took his arm and left him with almost no memory of what exactly happened that day. He woke up in the hospital missing both his memory and an appendage, with nary a clue as to what really occured that fateful morning. And now the beach has been roped off to the public, so he can't even investigate!

With the beach closed for good, Finn has bigger fish to fry—like figuring out why strange things are happening all over **Harbor City**. People are suddenly becoming violent and animals are starting to mutate into bizarre and dangerous beasts. Something weird is happening on the island, and Finn's gonna get to the bottom of it!

Finneus is kind and loyal, with an unrivaled sense of adventure. He's not very bright, but he doesn't let that bother him (and he probably wouldn't understand if you were making fun of him, anyway). Despite being a bit of a dummy, he has a curious spirit and loves to explore. Any second not spent outside is a waste of time in his book!

Finn's fairly balanced stats make him a solid asset in battle. His **strength** and **defense** are reliably sturdy, and his sky-high **guts** level means he often lands criticals. He's capable of learning the most basic spells, but his low **magic** makes them essentially useless in all but the most dire circumstances. To make up for his measly magic capabilities and average muscle, he's capable of learning deadly physical techniques. At higher levels, he gains especially useful light-based techs and special moves.

LIKES: eating, the arcade, cool-looking rocks

DISLIKES: crowded beaches, odd mushrooms, books without pictures

PENELOPE

STATS

WEAPON: WATER GUNS

STRENGTH ●●●●●●●●●●●●

SPEED ●●●●●●●●●●●●

DEFENSE ●●●●●●●●●●●●

GUTS ●●●●●●●●●●●●

MAGIC ●●●●●●●●●●●●

LUCK ●●●●●●●●●●●●

AFFINITIES

FIRE	WATER	LIGHTNING	WIND	DEBUFFS	SHADOW	LIGHT
B-	A	C+	C	C-	D	B+

BIO

Penelope is Finn's best friend and the one who found him unconscious on the sand after the accident. She pushed him all the way to the hospital in an abandoned shopping cart, surely saving his life in the process. Finn was unconscious for days, but she never left his side.

She used to run the seaside snack bar, but with the beach closed down, who's gonna buy her world-famous seaweed ice cream? Finn loves to remind her that nobody bought her ice cream even when the beach *was* open, because who wants green savory ice cream? Perhaps some time off is just what Penelope needs to perfect her recipe, and maybe even come up with some new flavors! Or maybe it's time to let that dream die...

Penelope is clever, optimistic, and reliable, even if she gets sick of playing sidekick all the time. She knows she's destined for greatness and she'll stop at nothing to achieve her goals! She's extremely competitive, and has been known to black out entirely in the heat of an argument.

In battle, Penelope's **speed** and **range** are her greatest assets. Her respectable **magic** stat means most mid-level spells are available to her. Her superb agility makes her a perfect healer, if you choose to go that route. But that doesn't mean she's not an exceptional fighter as well! Her water gun can hit flying enemies that Finn and the others can't reach, and she can sometimes get two separate attacks in each round if you're facing a particularly slow enemy. Plus, her high **luck** means enemies often miss her and status attacks don't always land. Just because her physical stats aren't that high doesn't mean she's weak, and you're actually super rude for assuming so.

LIKES: fried jellyfish, thinking about aliens, beating Finn at video games

DISLIKES: bullies, seagulls, centipedes, getting up early

KNOX

STATS

STRENGTH	●●●●●●●○○○	
DEFENSE	●●●○○○○○○○	
MAGIC	●○○○○○○○○○	

SPEED	●○○○○○○○○○	
GUTS	●●●●●○○○○○	
LUCK	●●○○○○○○○○	

OCKEY STICKS

AFFINITIES

FIRE	WATER	NING	WIND	DEBUFFS	SHADOW	LIGHT
F	F	F	F	F	F	F

BIO

Why are kids going missing at **Persimmon Prep**? Knox was expelled for fighting before he could figure it out. Maybe with the help of Finn and his friends, he can finally uncover this bizarre conspiracy once and for all. Could the missing kids be connected to the other weird things happening around town?

Knox is brave, hotheaded, and more than a little clumsy. He used to be the captain of the hockey team before getting booted from school—but he swears he was just defending some scrawny nerd from a group of bullies who recently enrolled as exchange students. He tried explaining himself to the dean, but he just can't seem to express himself without screaming his head off. He's just passionate, that's all! And maybe he has some underlying rage issues, but that's neither here nor there. Knox is easily distracted and stubborn as an ox, but somewhere deep inside is a kind heart (though he'd never admit it).

During battles, Knox acts as both the rock *and* the hard place. Forget packing a punch, Knox is a suitcase full of knuckle sandwiches! His high **defense** makes him practically invincible to standard attacks, though he's terribly weak to spells and status ailments. He's also slow, meaning he's usually the last person attacking during any given round. But with proper buffs and techniques, he can be the deciding factor in a tough battle. Knox can help cover weaker allies and easily clobber groups of enemies with a hefty sweep of his hockey stick.

LIKES: hockey, cute boys, barbecue pizza (with extra onions)

DISLIKES: school, rain, homework, being made to feel stupid

CLAUDETTE

STATS

WEAPON: MUSIC

STRENGTH		SPEED
DEFENSE		UTS
MAGIC		LUCK

AFFINITIES

FIRE	WATER	LIGHTNING	WIND	DEBUFFS	SHADOW	LIGHT
B	B	B	B	B	B	B

BIO

Claudette is the reigning champ of **Yodel Cove Karaoke Bar**. But after winning the past three years' championships in a row, she's grown weary of the throne. With nobody left to challenge, she's abdicated her royal duties and taken the show on the road!

A born leader, Claudette is assertive, energetic, and just a *liiiiittle* bit bossy. But she's also sweet and empathetic, and she'd never lead her friends astray. That said, she has no time for whiners or people who don't pull their weight, and she'll see right through you if you try to pull any funny business.

Claudette is confident and fearless, making her handy in battle. She can swing her microphone at enemies for a fair amount of damage, but her real value lies in her singing voice. She can learn a variety of songs from different **cassette tapes** you acquire, allowing her to lull enemies to sleep or invigorate your party. Some tapes can be purchased in shops, but others can only be found on your travels. Her **magic** stat is decent, so she can fill in as a mage or healer, too!

LIKES: cool jams, vintage stickers, and being the center of attention whenever humanly possible

DISLIKES: yogurt, sand, dogs with bad breath

ESTHER

STATS

WEAPON: PROJECTILES

STRENGTH	SPEED
DEFENSE	GUTS
MAGIC	LUCK

AFFINITIES

FIRE	WATER	LIGHTNING	WIND	DEBUFFS	SHADOW	LIGHT
B	B	B	B	B	A+	F

BIO

Esther used to work at **Unlucky Peach** in the mall, but she got ~~fired~~ *I QUIT!* *I wasn't fired,*
for telling customers they had terrible style. *Well they did!!*

Now, she spends most of her time poring over occult magazines
and hunting cryptids, even though she hasn't found any yet. *???*
OK, and? That doesn't mean they aren't real!

The night before Finn's accident, she swears she had a premonition
about something (bad happening) on the island, and she just can't
seem to shake the feeling that it's only going to get (worse.) *IT IS!!*
I DID! I SWEAR!!!

Esther's prized possession is her limited edition **Pigaru fannypack.**
In fact, she's the only one in the world who owns one, because she's
the only person who bought one. Because it's ugly.
UR JUST JEALOUS! ☺ ~~×~~ *SHUT UP IT IS NOT!*

Despite how (hideous) her fannypack is, it appears to be magic.
No matter how much trash she puts inside of it, it never seems to fill
up. She can store as many items as the party needs inside, plus
numerous projectiles to use in battle, like marbles, paper airplanes,
and bottle rockets. *AND A GUN (MAYBE)*

STOP BEING MEAN

Esther has the highest **magic** in the group, making her the de facto
spellcaster, as she's the only one who can learn high-level spells. *Thank you*
She can also use powerful projectiles, but they're single-use items
and can get very expensive.

LIKES: spiky pear soda, cataloguing her Pigaru figurines, old horror
movies

DISLIKES: mayonnaise, her parents, you probably
True.

THEODORE (AND TORTELLINI)

STATS

WEAPON: WHISTLES

STRENGTH	●●○○○○○○○○	
DEFENSE	●●●●○○○○○○	
MAGIC	●●●●●○○○○○	

SPEED	●●●●●●●○○○	
GUTS	●●●○○○○○○○	
LUCK	●●●●●○○○○○	

AFFINITIES

FIRE	WATER	LIGHTNING	WIND	DEBUFFS	SHADOW	LIGHT
C+	B	B-	A	C+	D+	B

BIO

Theodore is a thoughtful and gentle soul who runs a little animal clinic out of his backyard. Other kids say he can actually talk to animals, but that's not really true—critters just like him a lot! He doesn't have many friends, but that's just because he's usually too busy tending to injured birds and squirrels.

His parents are both biologists who are stationed far up north studying ice microbes, so he lives with his grandmother **Ruby**. She's always baking something tasty, so be sure to stop by for a visit!

Theo's best friend is his dog **Tortellini**, who sadly died in a car accident but decided he wasn't quite ready to pass on and stuck around as a ghost. And that's just as well, because Theo would rather not get involved in scuffles if possible. Instead, he can summon Tortellini into battle to fight in his stead. Tortellini can even learn new **tricks** if you discover certain rare items. Plus, Theo can summon other animals if he has the right **whistle** equipped. Make sure to collect them all and develop a formidable animal army!

LIKES: animals of all sorts, science books, his grandmother's purple carrot tarts

DISLIKES: being the center of attention

TOWN
INFO

Harbor City is the biggest city on the islands. Always bustling with people, it's the commercial center of Toro Island. There's always something to do and the merchants there constantly get new items in stock, so make sure to visit the city often!

IMOGEN
INFO

Imogen runs a junk shop in town. Aptly called **Imogen's Scrapyard**, it's your go-to stop for weapons and gear. You can also bring her raw materials to improve the weapons you already have, boosting their attack power. Imogen is a little gruff, but she's friendly enough. She also loves vintage bodybuilding magazines, so if you run across any, be sure to hand them over in exchange for permanent discounts in her shop!

PALOMA
INFO

Paloma operates a teeny magic shop, selling all sorts of curious baubles and useful accessories. She's usually deep in thought concocting new spells, so you might have to ring the bell at the front desk a couple times before she notices you. Paloma will sell you all sorts of beginner spells, but make sure your magic stat is high enough to learn the desired spell. Like her wife, Imogen, Paloma loves to collect things, so if you find any sparkly crystals in your travels, bring them to her for permanent discounts!

IMOGEN AND PALOMA

Buy Equipment
Improve Gear
Give Magazine

Buy Magic
Buy Accessories
Give Crystal

FELIX AND FLAX

Buy Medicine
Sell Items
Give B'caps

FELIX

Felix is a trainee pharmacist at **Harbor City Hypermarket**. He's still learning, so please be patient with him! Felix is easily flustered, but there's nobody in the whole city who's more knowledgable about medicinal science. Come to him for all your curative needs, and if you're lucky, he'll have a few special items in stock that can't be found anywhere else!

FLAX

Flax is Felix's pet cat. She can usually be found dozing in his lap (when she's not batting pill bottles off shelves). If you give her a pet, you'll get a tiny boost to all your stats for the next five battles! Flax loves to collect **bottle caps**, so if you bring her enough of them, something good might happen!

ITEM001-003

BOTTLES, ETC.

NOVA COLA   INFO

A bottle of strange (but delicious!) soda that seems to defy gravity. Use it in battle for a temporary strength boost. Once used, the empty bottle and its cap are added back to your inventory.

EMPTY BOTTLE   INFO

These empty bottles can be found in trash cans or floating in the ocean. Throw them in battle for moderate damage, or trade 'em in at a recycling center for prizes!

BOTTLE CAP   INFO

These might seem like common junk, but they're very precious to certain people! One man's trash is actually Flax's prized possession. Make sure to hold on to them and hand them over. You might get rewarded in the future! Or you might not! It's impossible to tell!

GUMMIES

Buy Gummies
Mix Gummies
Bash Machine

VENDING MACHINES

INFO

These vending machines can be found all over the island!
You can purchase all types of gummies from them, or even
make your own. Experiment with different ingredients to
create more powerful and interesting gummies! You can
also bang on the machine and sometimes get free items,
but if you do it too often the machine might break for good!

APPLE GUMMY INFO

Restores a small amount of HP to a single party member.

PEACH GUMMY INFO

Restores a moderate amount of HP to a single party member.

MELON GUMMY INFO

Fully restores the HP of a single party member.

BLUEBERRY GUMMY INFO

Restores a moderate amount of HP to all party members.

SEA SALT GUMMY INFO

Fully restores all HP to all party members and removes status ailments.

LUNAR MILK GUMMY INFO

Revives a fainted party member and restores half of their HP.

GRILLED GUMMY INFO

A piping hot gummy! Temporarily adds fire element to attacks.

SNOWY GUMMY INFO

A chilly gummy! Brr! Temporarily adds ice element to attacks.

MOSSY GUMMY INFO

Made from the moss of a high mountain. Adds wind element to attacks.

ELECTRIC GUMMY INFO

Not for the faint of heart! Adds electricity to your attacks.

SESAME GUMMY INFO

A pitch-black, savory gummy that frankly tastes awful. Adds shadow element to attacks.

LUMINOUS GUMMY INFO

This gummy is somehow tasteless and weightless in your mouth! Adds light element to attacks.

STATUS CONDITIONS

DARK INFO

With impaired vision, a character can't see their target and becomes unable to land physical hits until cured.

SILENCE INFO

A silenced ally becomes voiceless, making it impossible to cast spells until the situation is remedied.

POISON INFO

A poisoned party turns a sickly green and slowly loses health over an extended period of time.

DREAMY INFO

A character who is asleep cannot move or input any commands. Wake them up with a swift bonk!

CURSED INFO

If cursed, a character takes damage from healing spells. They also won't receive EXP at the end of the battle.

BLESSED INFO

A blessed ally's HP regenerates slowly over time, and any healing spells they cast restore additional HP.

CONFUSED INFO

A confused party member can't tell friend from foe, and attacks indiscriminately.

FAINTED INFO

If someone's HP drops to zero, they will faint and no longer be usable in battle unless they're revived.

FRENZIED INFO

If your character enters a frenzy, they become much faster and stronger, but you lose control of them.

SLOW INFO

An ally inflicted with slow becomes sluggish, and they won't be able to act as often in battle.

PUMPED UP INFO

Certain items and spells can temporarily boost different stats, but the effect wears off after several turns.

FROG INFO

A rare status ailment where you are tranformed into a frog, decreasing your strength and defense.

CURATIVES

FRESHMINT INFO

Restores a small
amount of MP to a
single party member.

CINNAMINT INFO

Restores a moderate
amount of MP to a
single party member.

WINTERMINT INFO

Restores a very small
amount of MP to all
party members.

STARMINT INFO

Restores a moderate
amount of MP to all
party members.

CHERRY LOZENGE INFO

Cures **poison** for
one party member.

HONEY LOZENGE INFO

Cures **poison** for
all party members.

CURATIVES

GINKGO INFO

Cures **dark** for one party member.

GINSENG INFO

Cures **silence** for one party member.

FISH OIL INFO

Cures **slow** for one party member.

SMELLING SALTS INFO

Awakens a sleeping party member from a **dreamy slumber** and occasionally boosts speed and accuracy.

ALOE INFO

This fresh chunk of aloe cures a party member who has been **frenzied**.

DEWDROPS INFO

This sweet candy made from purified pond water cures **frog** status.

CHAMOMILE INFO

Fragrant and delicious tea that cures **curse** in one party member.

LEVEL 1 WEAPONS

OAK BAT
FINN

A simple but sturdy bat for beginners.
Delivers light, blunt damage.

ATK: 20 | **MAG:** 5 | **CRIT:** 10% | **ELEMENT:** none

BARRACUDA
PENELOPE

A basic water gun. Enemies that are
weak to water take extra damage!

ATK: 14 | **MAG:** 17 | **CRIT:** 8% | **ELEMENT:** water

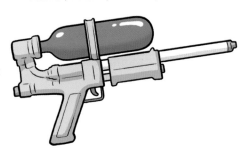

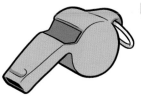

POP JAMZ
CLAUDETTE

A collection of upbeat songs that boost
the party's offense and defense.

ATK: 12 | **MAG:** 22 | **CRIT:** 5% | **ELEMENT:** none

PLASTIC WHISTLE
THEODORE

A flimsy whistle from a vending
machine. Summons a swarm of
rats to claw at enemies.

ATK: 13 | **MAG:** 10 | **CRIT:** 9% | **ELEMENT:** none

OAK STICK
KNOX

A hockey stick stolen from the gym at
Persimmon Prep. Strong but boring
(sort of like Knox).

ATK: 30 | **MAG:** 0 | **CRIT:** 10% | **ELEMENT:** none

BEGINNER
SPELLS
for
YOUNG
WITCHES

BEGINNER
SPELLBOOK
ESTHER

A spellbook for beginners "borrowed"
from Unlucky Peach. Contains simple
elemental and healing spells.

ATK: 0 | **MAG:** 30 | **CRIT:** n/a | **ELEMENT:** n/a

★STARFISH★ BEACH

DUNGEON

Once, Starfish Beach was the premier vacation destination for tourists and locals alike. But the near death of a local teenager caused the entire beach to shut down until further notice. There are plenty of rumors about what happened, but nobody knows for sure. Maybe if you sneak past the barricades you can uncover clues...

EN001-002
BEACH ENEMIES

FIZZPOP TYPE: ARTIFICIAL

A weird little sentient ice pop lookin' for trouble. Uses extremely weak fire attacks and doesn't pose much of a threat.

HP: 20 | **MP:** 15
WEAK: everything | **IMMUNE:** n/a

BOMB PAPA TYPE: ARTIFICIAL

A terrifying elder ice pop who only appears after you've killed **one hundred Fizzpops**. Extremely dangerous, so be careful about encountering these fellas!

HP: 500 | **MP:** 150
WEAK: n/a | **IMMUNE:** blind

STAR CRASHER TYPE: BEAST

A fearless starfish with zero regard for either your life or its own. When its health is low, it crashes into your party, killing itself and damaging you with a fiery explosion.

HP: 40 | **MP:** 10
WEAK: n/a | **IMMUNE:** n/a

STARFISH TYPE: BEAST

A rambunctious little sea star whose bark is bigger than its bite. Kicks up clumps of sand and occasionally takes breaks to cry.

HP: 20 | **MP:** 0
WEAK: fire | **IMMUNE:** n/a

FIRESTAR TYPE: BEAST

A hotheaded starfish who hurls fireballs from afar. Give it a blast with Penelope's water gun and it'll become harmless.

HP: 30 | **MP:** 10
WEAK: water | **IMMUNE:** fire

ZAPFISH TYPE: BEAST

A speedy, slippery fiend that lurks in the shallow waters of the beach. They can be quite tough, but you're safe as long as you keep away from the water. If you're feeling bold, you might get a tasty eel fillet out of the ordeal!

HP: 150 | **MP:** 75
WEAK: physical | **IMMUNE:** lightning

ITEM029
EEL FILLET INFO

A scrumptious, sushi-grade slab of fresh eel! Tastes great but numbs your mouth. Use it in battle to boost your electric resistance, or transform it into **electric gummies**.

RUSTY HELMET

RUSTY HELMET TYPE: BEAST

An old rusty helmet that's washed ashore. It won't move or attack you no matter how much you pummel it. Give it a few good whacks and see what happens!

HP: 30 | **MP:** 0 | **WEAK:** n/a | **IMMUNE:** n/a

SHELLFISH TYPE: BEAST

What's this??? A vicious, mutated crab! Once you've depleted the helmet's HP, its true form is revealed. These crabs attack with swift pinching attacks and blast you with noxious bubbles. If you're not quick enough, it might pop back into its shell, and you'll need to bash it a few more times to coax it back out.

HP: 90 | **MP:** 55
WEAK: fire | **IMMUNE:** water

MEDUSAE TYPE: HYBRID

Who was this poor, unfortunate soul before this startling transformation took place? A large jellyfish has taken control of her senses, and now she aimlessly stumbles along the desolate beach, mindlessly hunting for prey. She attacks with lacerating tentacle whips and uses potent lighting magic when her health drops below 50%. Keep your wits about you and end her suffering!

HP: 500 | **MP:** 250 | **WEAK:** fire | **IMMUNE:** lighting, poison

MEDUSAE

..kill..kill......kill...............
........kill...............kill....
....................kill...............

PERSIMMON PREP

DUNGEON

Investigating **Starfish Beach** uncovered nothing new beyond confirming suspicions that something is very wrong on the island. With no real leads, there's nothing else to do but investigate other strange rumors, like the one at **Persimmon Preparatory Academy**. Right before summer break, a number of kids mysteriously went missing. After a student reported hearing odd groans from the gymnasium basement, the school year was abruptly ended early and the building was locked up tight. Perhaps you can find an open window and explore the abandoned school...?

EN008-009
SCHOOL ENEMIES

APPLE JACK   TYPE: PLANT

He's one bad apple! It's not clear if he's a student who transformed, or a particularly ambitious apple who gained sentience. Both he and the worms in his head are capable of attacking, so watch out!

HP: 60 | **MP:** 0
WEAK: fire | **IMMUNE:** n/a

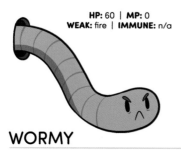

WORMY   TYPE: BUG

This weak little worm is more of an annoyance than anything, but they can overwhelm you if you're not careful. They have a pitiful amount of HP, so a quick AoE spell or technique can eradicate them quickly.

HP: 1 | **MP:** 0 | **WEAK:** very much so | **IMMUNE:** n/a

SKYROCKET
TYPE: ARTIFICIAL

A small, angry shuttlecock, usually found in groups of three or six. Not very strong but deadly in large number!

HP: 20 | **MP:** 30
WEAK: n/a | **IMMUNE:** n/a

GREAT DODGER
TYPE: ARTIFICIAL

A large and lazy dodgeball that evades physical attacks unless you have high luck. It can't dodge magic, though!

HP: 200 | **MP:** 40
WEAK: sleep | **IMMUNE:** dark

WATCHER
TYPE: ARTIFICIAL

A grotesque mutated baseball that can pinpoint your weakness and use appropriate magic spells. Dies instantly if whacked with a bat.

HP: 50 | **MP:** 150
WEAK: bats | **IMMUNE:** dark

Milky™
TYPE: ???

A cute little carton from **Milky Corp.**, a huge donor of Persimmon Prep. It might not actually be milk? It just wants to be friends. Toss it some **milk money** for some easy XP!

HP: 2 | **MP:** 0 | **WEAK:** n/a | **IMMUNE:** n/a

ROTTEN *Milky*™
TYPE: ???

If you attack Milky, it will transform into Rotten Milky! It uses toxic attacks to poison your party. The more you attack, the angrier it gets, before finally exploding and damaging your whole party.

HP: 90 | **MP:** 50 | **WEAK:** fire | **IMMUNE:** poison

SCHOOL ENEMIES

BAD EGG
TYPE: BEAST

A disgusting mutant egg who hides amongst fresh eggs. You'll just have to keep smashing eggs by attacking them until you find the real culprit!

HP: Egg: 1 / Bad Egg: 50 | **MP:** 0 | **WEAK:** n/a | **IMMUNE:** n/a
DROPS: Lucky Peach, Crystal Peach (rare)

ITEM030
LUCKY PEACH
INFO

A succulent, juicy peach! Use it in battle to raise everyone's **luck** a little bit, increasing accuracy and improving the chances of receiving rare loot.

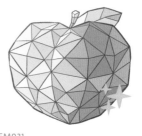

ITEM031
CRYSTAL PEACH
INFO

What a gorgeous peach! It's totally inedible, but it's so shiny! Use it in battle to double the amount of XP earned.

FISHMONGER MABEL
TYPE: HUMAN

Mabel used to run a popular seafood emporium, providing delectable cuts of fish to the elite student body of Persimmon Prep. Over time, mercury poisoning has been slowly driving her insane, recently accelerated by some nefarious force. Now, she's looking for new dishes to serve...like children, perhaps? But who exactly is she cooking for? Maybe you don't want to find out...

HP: 750 | **MP:** 0 | **WEAK:** fire, lightning | **IMMUNE:** water, poison | **DROPS:** Basement Key

BOSS002
FISHMONGER MABEL

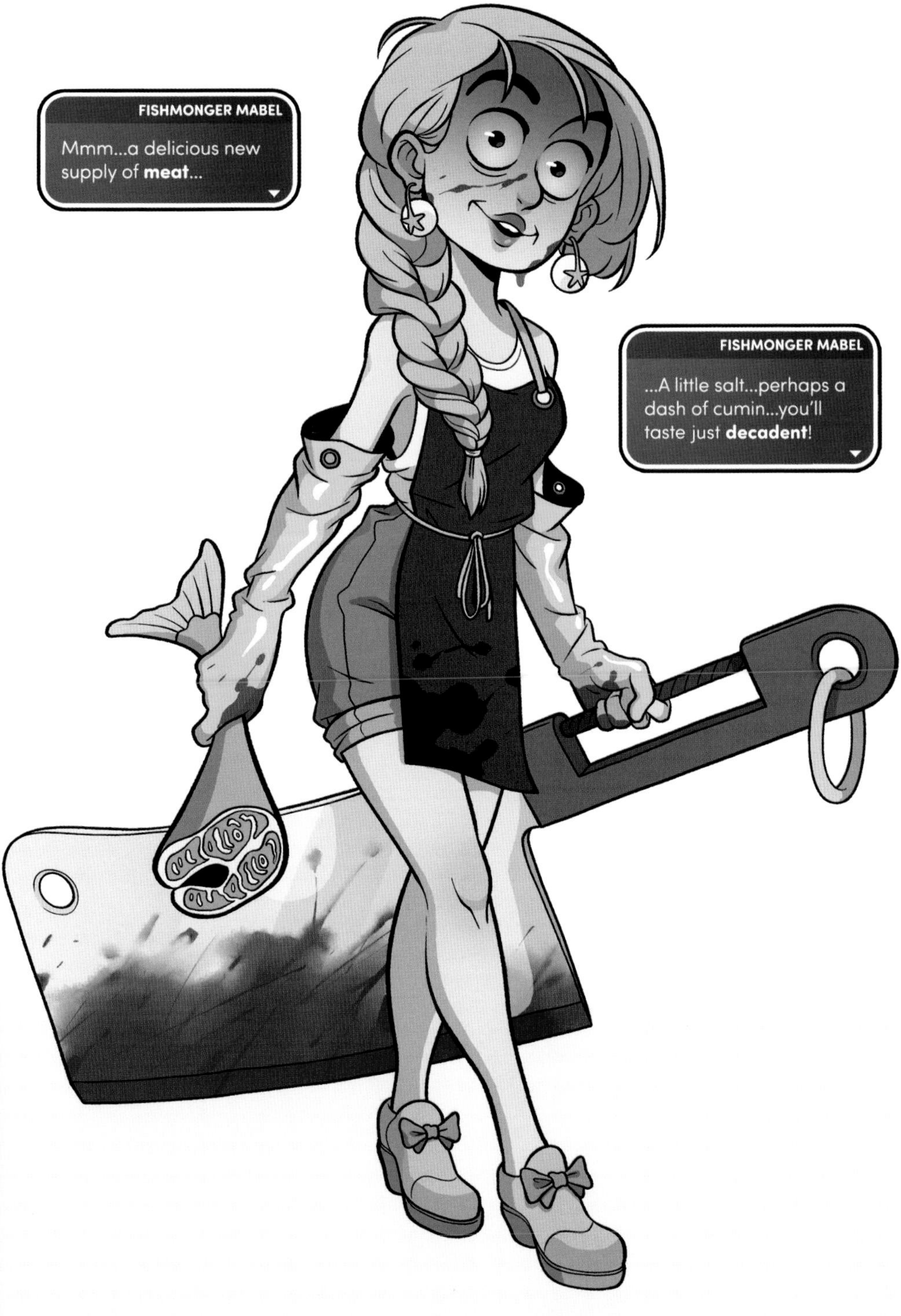
FISHMONGER MABEL
Mmm...a delicious new supply of **meat**...
FISHMONGER MABEL
...A little salt...perhaps a dash of cumin...you'll taste just **decadent**!

BASEMENT KEY

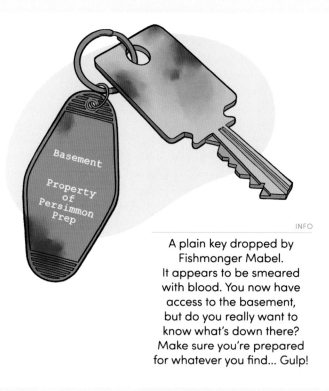

INFO

A plain key dropped by
Fishmonger Mabel.
It appears to be smeared
with blood. You now have
access to the basement,
but do you really want to
know what's down there?
Make sure you're prepared
for whatever you find... Gulp!

THE HUNGER
TYPE: ???

Deep in the basement, hidden from view, a bizarre mass of undulating goo oozes about, consuming anything and everything in its path. Is this what was making those sinister groans? Or was it perhaps someone caught by this horrific being, screaming as they were slowly devoured? And where did such a monster come from? All of this remains a mystery, but one thing is clear: whatever creature this is, it wants nothing more than to swallow you whole!

The Hunger is a formidable foe, using its slimy hands to pull weapons out of itself to use in battle. It can also shoot ooze-covered balls at you, so keep your defense up! Every now and then it will gobble up a member of your party, removing them from battle for a few turns before spitting them back out (perhaps they weren't seasoned well enough?).

HP: 1,550 | **MP:** 0 | **WEAK:** fire, slow | **IMMUNE:** poison, blind

THE HUNGER

THE HUNGER

Grriuug...hghhh.....grghl
grurrrrr.....ghhhhhh.........
ggrghgghGRGGGGHHH

MYSTERIOUS GIRL

AMELIA

Don't try running, Finn!
I'll track you down no
matter where you go!

AMELIA

TYPE: HUMAN

Having cleared Persimmon Prep, Finneus and his friends leave out the back of the
school, only to be intercepted by a mysterious girl with a vicious grudge. Who is she,
and where does she come from? And why is she hell-bent on killing Finn at all costs?
Amelia will impede your progress every so often. She'll always run off right before
you best her, only to come back stronger than before. In battle she's swift and
aggressive, so keep an eye on your HP and with a little luck you'll prevail!

HP: 1,111 | **MP:** 111 | **WEAK:** lightning, slow | **IMMUNE:** poison, dark

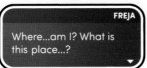

FREJA

Where...am I? What is this place...?

BIO

In a secluded clearing beyond the school, a strange girl lies unconscious.

When Freja awakens, she can't remember anything. She knows she's not of this world, but she can't remember where she's from or how long she's been here. Nor can she recall why she's bound in chains. But perhaps Finn and his friends can help her unravel the truth.

Sensing peculiar strength in Finn's group, Freja sends them on a quest. She feels the presence of several mystical treasures scattered across the island. If Finn and his friends can retrieve them, they might unlock certain **hidden powers**...and possibly help Freja remember her past. She feels energies coming from six locations...

★ Anarchy has broken out at a popular **fast food restaurant** in town...

★ Low tides have revealed a **strange cave** at the Starfish Beach...

★ Though the evil has been extinguished at Persimmon Prep, a deadly but stylish gang of **new students** has taken over amidst the chaos...

★ A local band is causing a commotion at a **grimy theater** downtown...

★ An abandoned **theme park** outside the city has suddenly opened for business...

★ Locals are reporting strange sounds coming from **Theodore's house**. Is his grandmother Ruby alright...?

You can tackle these quests in any order you wish. Good luck!

BOK BOK CHICKEN SHACK

DUNGEON

Bok Bok Chicken Shack is Harbor City's most popular fast food restaurant. They serve the most delicious chicken* on the whole island. **_It's a cluckin' good time!™_** Or at least it used to be. Chaos has broken out in recent days. Employees are becoming hostile, food is coming to life and attacking patrons, and there are horrible noises coming from the back room. What's going on at Bok Bok?

*The chicken served at Bok Bok Chicken Shack is 51% chicken, which means it can legally be called chicken. The other 49% is none of your business. Patent pending.

EN016A-016B
MILKSHAKE

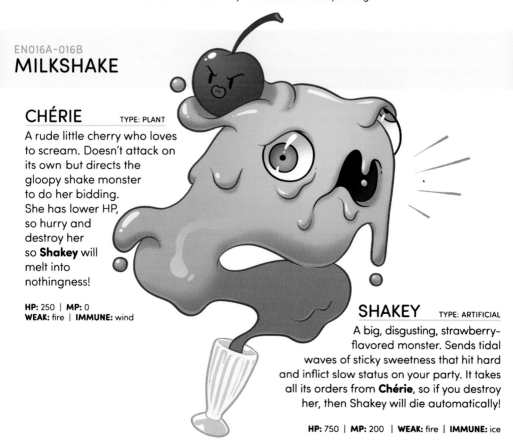

CHÉRIE   TYPE: PLANT

A rude little cherry who loves to scream. Doesn't attack on its own but directs the gloopy shake monster to do her bidding. She has lower HP, so hurry and destroy her so **Shakey** will melt into nothingness!

HP: 250 | **MP:** 0
WEAK: fire | **IMMUNE:** wind

SHAKEY   TYPE: ARTIFICIAL

A big, disgusting, strawberry-flavored monster. Sends tidal waves of sticky sweetness that hit hard and inflict slow status on your party. It takes all its orders from **Chérie**, so if you destroy her, then Shakey will die automatically!

HP: 750 | **MP:** 200 | **WEAK:** fire | **IMMUNE:** ice

BOK BOK SOLDIER

SOLDIER

TYPE: HUMAN

A part-time soldier. Will cut you as soon as look at you. Very dangerous when they aren't distracted, and especially intimidating in larger groups.

HP: 120 | **MP:** 10 **WEAK:** wind | **IMMUNE:** fire
DROPS: Chicky Burgers, Chicky Fries, Bok Boxes (rare)

ITEM033-037
FAST FOOD

CHICKY FRIES INFO

Use in battle to boost a party member's magic, but it also lowers their magic defense.

PIGARU CHARM INFO

A small, adorable accessory. Equip it to raise each stat by 2. Neat!

CHICKY BURGER INFO

A juicy burger! Doubles your HP in battle but also causes slow.

BOK BOX INFO

A full meal! Contains a Chicky Burger, a side of fries, and a toy! If you're lucky, you might get a rare Pigaru Charm!

DELUXE PIGARU CHARM INFO

A rare Pigaru charm plated in gold. Raises each stat by 5. Wow!

BOK BOK

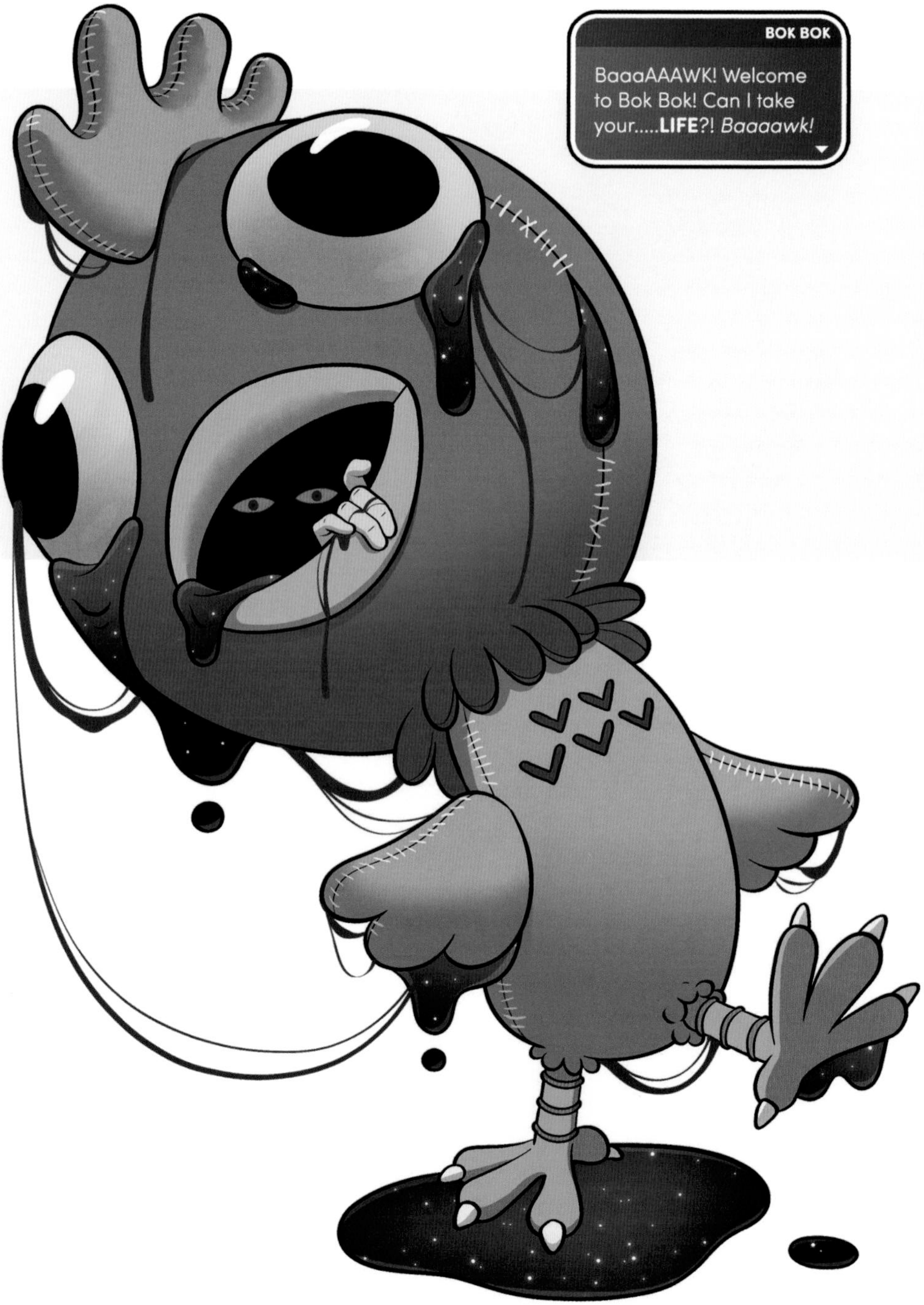
BOK BOK
BaaaAAAWK! Welcome to Bok Bok! Can I take your.....**LIFE**?! *Baaaawk!*

BOK BOK

Once a lovable mascot, Bok Bok has been transformed into a gruesome monster. A sickly gurgling can be heard coming from inside the costume. Why is it covered in the same **weird goop** as the creature in the basement of Persimmon Prep? They're obviously connected, but how?

Bok Bok can be a tough enemy, but its attacks are fairly straightforward. It runs around the battlefield crashing into your characters and occasionally hurls clumps of goo at you that cause mild shadow damage. It might be a long battle, but hang in there and you'll scrape by!

HP: 3,400 | **MP:** 30 | **WEAK:** light, lightning | **IMMUNE:** sleep, dark | **DROPS:** Royal Catalyst

ITEM038
ROYAL CATALYST
INFO

Though it appears to be an ordinary paper crown, it hums with the energy of a dying knight. How did it come to be infused with such curious power? Bring it to **Freja**, and perhaps she can make sense of it. It seems to radiate a particularly strong energy when Finn holds it. Perhaps it can be used to inspire a powerful evolution in his abilites?

HIDDEN ★ SEA ★ CAVES

DUNGEON

With the previously popular Starfish Beach now deserted, the sea levels have changed ever so slightly. Now, low tides have revealed an eerie cave system that was previously filled with water. Inside, peculiar creatures await, ready to attack trespassers. Stranger still is the myriad artifacts scattered about—wooden planks, bits of metal and old rope...

...the remains of a ship, perhaps?

EN018-019

CAVE ENEMIES

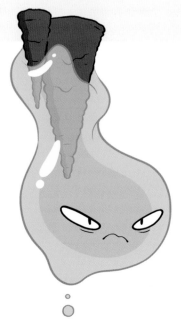

DRIPPY   TYPE: SLIME

A gelatinous slime mold who would love nothing more than to slowly devour you over the course of several months. Can only be reached with ranged attacks and magic, since it clings to the ceiling.

HP: 220 | **MP:** 0 | **WEAK:** fire | **IMMUNE:** poison

GOOPY   TYPE: SLIME

It's the same as Drippy but on the ground. It has somewhat higher defense, and it can't damage you directly, instead inducing **poison** to whittle away your health little by little.

HP: 220 | **MP:** 0 | **WEAK:** fire | **IMMUNE:** poison

CAVE ENEMIES

URCHIN ORPHAN
TYPE: HYBRID

A curious little urchin who's adapted to the pitch blackness of cave life. It uses a crude form of magic it created itself, and moves with erratic speed, evading attacks.

HP: 190 | **MP:** 300 | **WEAK:** n/a | **IMMUNE:** silence
DROPS: Sea Glass Fragments, Bone Fragments

FINTROOPER
TYPE: HYBRID

A mutated fish (or is it a mutated man?) with a long hook that can cause bleeding damage. They're fiercely territorial and often call on backup troops to join the fray, especially when their health is low.

HP: 200 | **MP:** 0 | **WEAK:** fire | **IMMUNE:** water | **DROPS:** Bone Fragments, Seashell Fragments

CAVE ITEMS

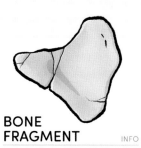

SEA GLASS FRAGMENT
INFO

A smooth, shiny piece of ocean glass. Used for crafting purposes.

BONE FRAGMENT
INFO

A chunk of bone from some unknown animal. Use it for crafting.

SEASHELL FRAGMENT
INFO

A broken segment of shell. Used to craft new equipment.

Imogen can use these raw materials to enhance your gear! Glass boosts magic power, bone fragments can improve physical attacks, and seashells can enhance accessories!

BOTTLE MERCHANT

SEAWEED GIRL   INFO

A little girl who wanders the beach outside the hidden caves at night and sorts through detritus washed up on the shore. She won't talk to you, but she will sell you empty bottles if you ask nicely—but not for cash. She doesn't seem to have any interest in actual money...

ITEM042
SAND DOLLAR   INFO

A simple shell, found all over the beach. Used as currency by some.

ITEM043
BOTTLE   INFO

A plain bottle. Nothing special!

ITEM044
OCEAN WATER   INFO

Fresh seawater! Toss it to cause moderate water damage.

ITEM045
MOON JELLY   INFO

A jellyfish in a bottle. Causes lightning damage.

ITEM046
MURKY WATER   INFO

Gross! Inflicts **dark** status.

DREAD PIRATE BONNIE   TYPE: UNDEAD

The famed pirate queen Bonnie Beatrix Baxter Byron was once the most feared marauder in the whole archipelago, until one day she vanished without a trace, never to be seen again. Now, something has brought her back from her watery grave, and she's got murder on her mind!

HP: 5,800 | **MP:** 350 | **WEAK:** healing magic/items | **IMMUNE:** water, poison | **DROPS:** Feather Catalyst

ITEM047
FEATHER CATALYST   INFO

A delicate, pristine feather from an unknown bird, imbued with the latent power of a dogged hunter. It bristles with energy when Penelope holds it. Take it to Freja ASAP!

DREAD PIRATE BONNIE

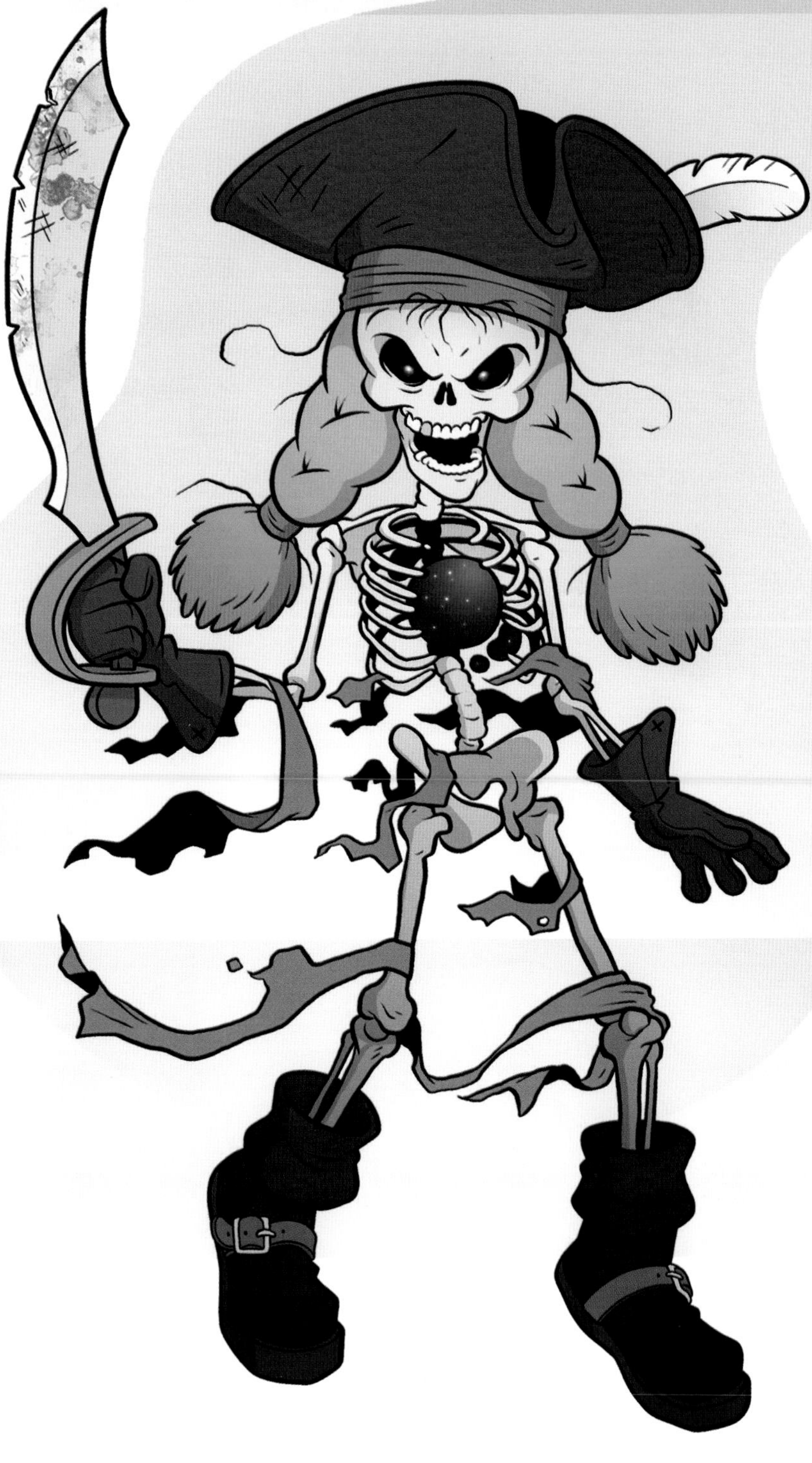

LEVEL 2 WEAPONS

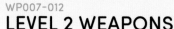

PIRANHA BAT   FINN

A bat made of salvaged wood, topped with a vicious biting fish skeleton!

ATK: 45 | **MAG:** 5 | **CRIT:** 15% | **ELEMENT:** none

RUM PUNCH   PENELOPE

An upgraded water gun with an old pirate bottle affixed to it.

ATK: 28 | **MAG:** 30 | **CRIT:** 15% | **ELEMENT:** water

OCEAN VIBES   CLAUDETTE

Chill ocean vibes, baby! Filled with songs that lull enemies to sleep and slow them down.

ATK: 22 | **MAG:** 40 | **CRIT:** 5% | **ELEMENT:** none

SIREN CALL   THEODORE

An old conch shell that summons seagulls to peck at enemies.

ATK: 23 | **MAG:** 39 | **CRIT:** 15% | **ELEMENT:** none

MR. TUSKY   KNOX

A hockey stick with a walrus tusk attachment. Adds very weak water damage to attacks.

ATK: 60 | **MAG:** 0 | **CRIT:** 10% | **ELEMENT:** water

PIRATE JOURNAL   ESTHER

A water-logged journal that belonged to a pirate. Contains purported mermaid lore and simple water spells.

ATK: 0 | **MAG:** 60 | **CRIT:** n/a | **ELEMENT:** n/a

CALAMITY CLUB

BOSSES

INFO

Oh, you thought you were done with **Persimmon Prep**? It's cute that you believed that! In the ensuing chaos following the revelation of the missing kids, a new gang has seized power. They call themselves the **Calamity Club**. The different members can be tackled in any order, but you'll have to defeat all three if you want to save the school once and for all!

BOSS007

ROCCIA

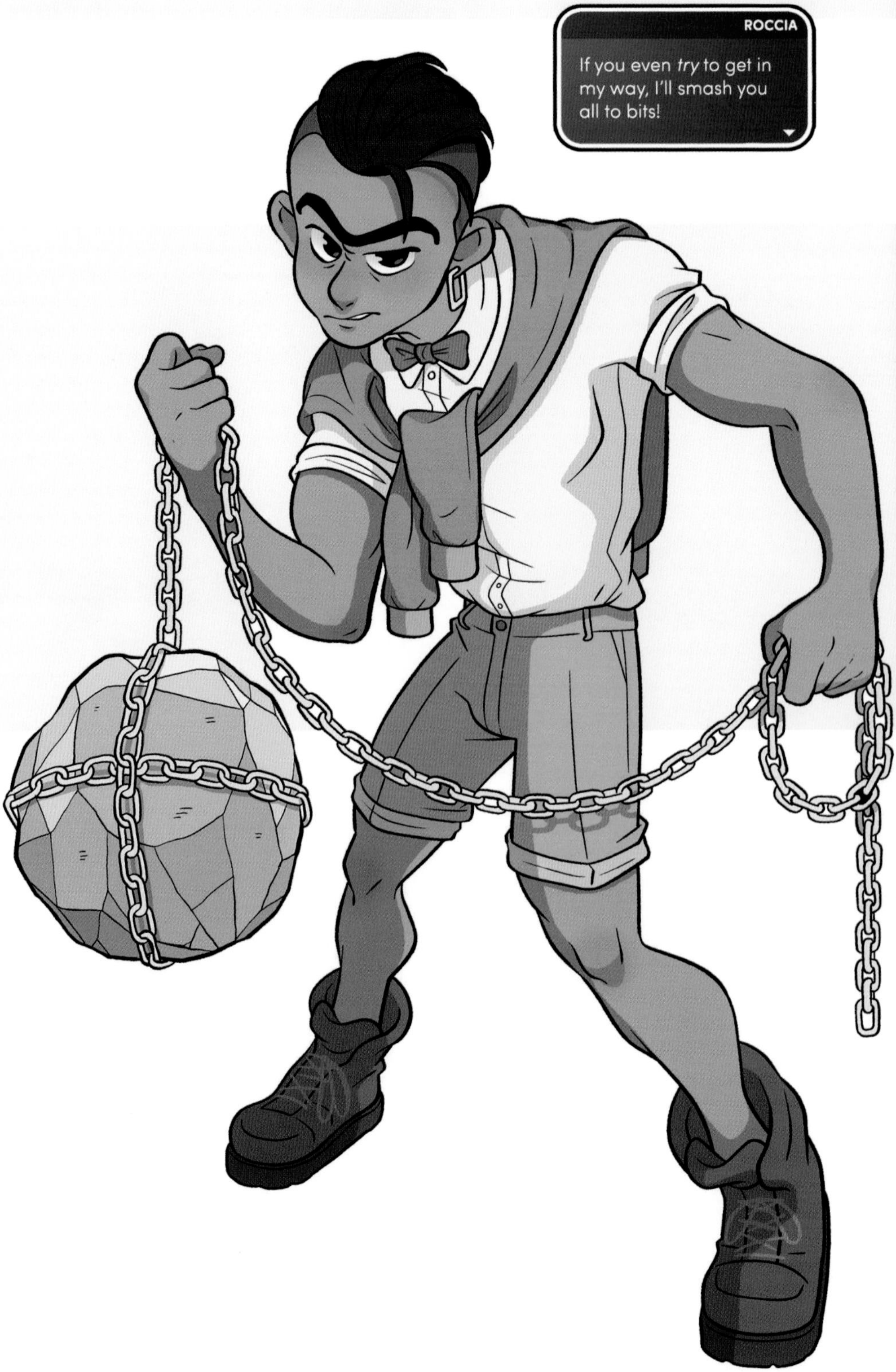
ROCCIA
If you even *try* to get in my way, I'll smash you all to bits!

ROCCIA

TYPE: HUMAN

Roccia only cares about one thing: *smashing stuff!* He can be found in the **science lab**, probably because it's full of glass beakers to destroy. Roccia is a complete numbskull and acts as Calamity Club's muscle, making him a difficult foe to vanquish. In battle, he swings his massive boulder around, which can KO you in one hit if you're under-leveled. Thankfully, he's quite slow and weak to magic. Plus, if **Penelope** is in your party, he'll periodically get distracted while staring longingly at her, causing him to miss a turn.

Once bested, Roccia will begrudgingly grant you his respect. In turn, he'll offer to teach **Knox** new fighting techniques, but only if Knox can beat him in solo combat.

HP: 7,654 | **MP:** 0 | **WEAK:** fire, ice, wind, lightning | **IMMUNE:** dark | **DROPS:** Silver Key

ITEM048
SILVER KEY
INFO

A plain silver key. It doesn't appear useful right now, but maybe it will be later?

BOSS008

KAMI

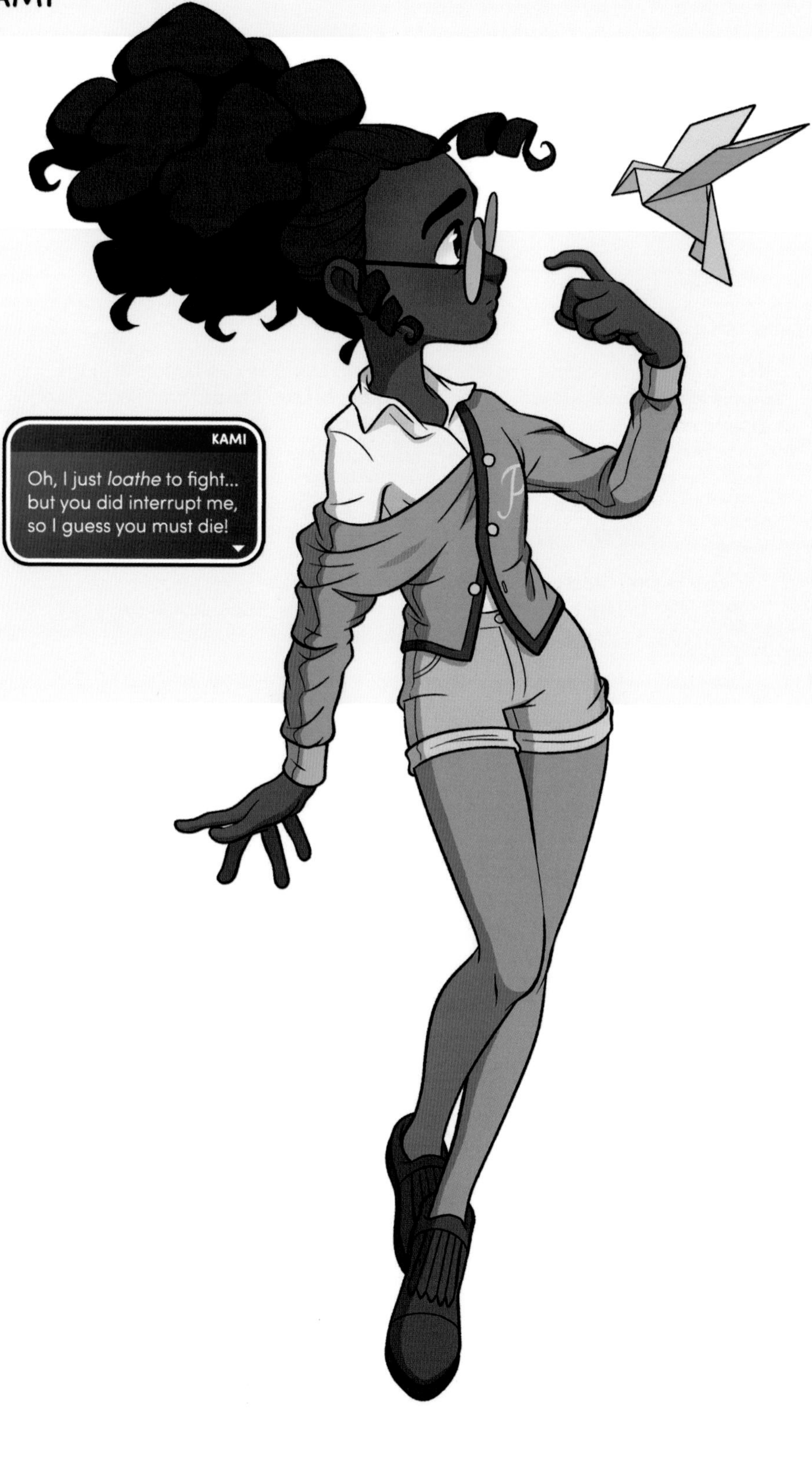
KAMI
Oh, I just *loathe* to fight...
but you did interrupt me,
so I guess you must die!

KAMI

TYPE: HUMAN

Kami always seems lost in thought, but don't let her dreamy demeanor fool you. If you intrude on one of her reveries, you might find yourself in the middle of a waking nightmare! You can find her in the **school library**, meandering through the stacks, humming some creepy song to herself. In battle she flings enchanted origami birds at you and attacks with powerful spells. She has no real weakness, so make sure you're well defended.

Once defeated, Kami will offer to teach you stronger mid-level spells. She also has several new powerful projectiles she'll sell to **Esther**.

HP: 5,678 | **MP:** 910 | **WEAK:** n/a | **IMMUNE:** silence, slow | **DROPS:** Gold Key

ITEM049
GOLD KEY
INFO

A plain gold key. It doesn't appear useful right now, but maybe it will be later?

CISEAUX

CISEAUX

I heard once that beauty is power—and *mon chou*, I have **ALL** the power!

CISEAUX

Always cool and calculating, Ciseaux is the leader of Calamity Club, and for good reason! They use twin scissor blades and attack with inhuman speed, so make sure you're ready before confronting them in the **principal's office**. When their health drops below 50%, they'll join their blades together into enormous shears that do even more damage.

After the battle is over, Ciseaux will reluctantly admit that you're the better warrior and offer to teach **Finn** some new fighting techniques—but only if your group has defeated enough enemies in combat. Check back periodically to see if they have some new stuff to teach you!

HP: 8,888 | **MP:** 0 | **WEAK:** poison | **IMMUNE:** dark, slow | **DROPS:** Old Lockbox

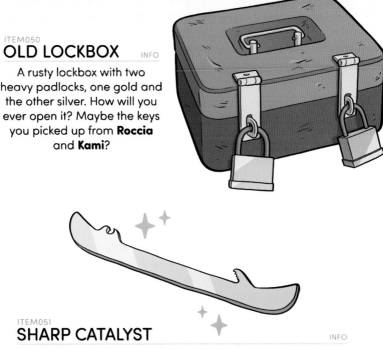

ITEM050
OLD LOCKBOX   INFO

A rusty lockbox with two heavy padlocks, one gold and the other silver. How will you ever open it? Maybe the keys you picked up from **Roccia** and **Kami**?

ITEM051
SHARP CATALYST   INFO

A golden hockey blade, found inside the rusty lockbox. It vibrates with the mighty essence of a decorated champion, now forgotten. It seems to glow when **Knox** holds it. Take it to **Freja** to unlock its true potential.

GOBLIN PALACE

DUNGEON

INFO

Goblin Palace is Harbor City's premier concert venue, attracting crust punks and glam rockers alike. It's noisy and grimy and that's just how the clientele likes it! But something's wrong at this beloved institution. Bizarre, atonal music is coming from inside, hypnotizing anyone who hears it and causing them to become violent and enraged. What could the commotion be? And how are you supposed to solve things if you can't get past the creepy music?

BOSS010
THE BOUNCER

AXEL RODD
TYPE: HUMAN

Axel Rodd (born Alexander Percival Roddrick II) is the bouncer at Goblin Palace, blocking entry of anyone he deems uncool. He's a failed musician with a *huge* chip on his shoulder, compounded by the fact that Goblin Palace barely pays above minimum wage. Not that it matters—his parents pay his rent, and they're both state senators. Not very punk, Axel!

He isn't the toughest foe, but he fights dirty and has a tendency to evade attacks. He'll also steal items from you if he gets a chance. If you want, you can bypass the battle altogether by **bribing** him for entry to the club.

HP: 6,969 | **MP:** 420 | **WEAK:** fire, a hundred dollars
IMMUNE: sleep | **DROPS:** Earplugs

CLUB ENEMIES

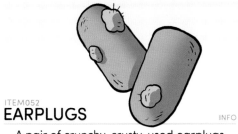

EARPLUGS
INFO

A pair of crunchy, crusty, used earplugs. They're disgusting, but at least they'll drown out the grotesque music in the club... Ugh!

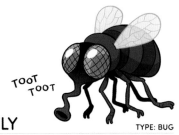

TOOT TOOT

BAR FLY
TYPE: BUG

A buzzy little nuisance that dodges most physical attacks. After a round or two, it will call on friends to join the fray.

HP: 175 | **MP:** 0 | **WEAK:** poison, magic | **IMMUNE:** slow

LIL' ROACH
TYPE: BUG

Look at this sneaky boy! He wants to bite ya!! He wants to steal ya coins!!! Squish him!!!!

HP: 310 | **MP:** 100 | **WEAK:** poison | **IMMUNE:** n/a

COILMASS
TYPE: ARTIFICIAL

A tangled cluster of audio cords gathered around a floating orb of glistening flesh. It alternates between fire, lightning, and ice magic. It's a wholly original creature—any resemblance to monsters from other games is purely coincidental.

HP: 400 | **MP:** 310 | **WEAK:** rotating spells | **IMMUNE:** dark, silence

NPC006
STARLA
INFO

Starla "runs" the Lost and Found at Goblin Palace. Or more accurately, she runs a shady racket out of the alley behind the club, selling forgotten items to anyone with a few bucks to spare. Everything she doesn't keep for herself is fair game, and she's happy to sell you some "gently used" accessories on the cheap.

ITEM053
SPIKY COLLAR
INFO

A totally stylish accessory! When it's equipped, any enemy that attacks you will take a small amount of damage in return.

ITEM054
ALLURING LIPSTICK
INFO

Gorgeous! It's missing the cap and it's been used, but it's probably still good? When equipped, your magic attack stat is raised by 10%.

ITEM055
CRACKED GLASSES
INFO

A less stylish accessory. When equipped, you become immune to **dark** and your resistance to all other status ailments is raised a little bit, too!

THE DISSONANCE

THE DISSONANCE

TYPE: ???

An imperceivable haze of sound and color, The Dissonance has no physical form to attack. It causes anyone who hears it to experience strange auditory hallucinations, both comforting and threatening in equal measure, until it eventually drives them insane. With no corporeal form to attack, how can it possibly be vanquished? There's no other choice but to fight fire with fire...

HP: n/a | **MP:** n/a | **WEAK:** n/a | **IMMUNE:** n/a | **DROPS:** Round Catalyst

BATTLE OF THE BANDS

ROCK ON!

The weird music at Goblin Palace can't be silenced with normal weapons, so what's a girl to do? Why, form the **greatest punk rock girl group** of all time, obviously!

The battle against The Dissonance functions as a **rhythm game**. Tap the corresponding buttons in time with the music, stringing together combos that damage the boss. If you get through the song without missing a beat, you'll impress the audience and get a cash bonus!

FUN TIP!

Starla has lots of outfits to choose from at the Lost and Found, but some are better than others! Choose digs that impress the audience, and you'll get a bigger bonus at the end!

FUN TIP!

Whichever outfits you choose become variant costumes for your characters through the rest of your journey. Radical!

ITEM056
ROUND CATALYST

INFO

A shiny, round disc with corrupted data. Though unreadable, it buzzes with vitality, especially around **Claudette**. Bring it to **Freja** to figure it out!

TICKET TAKER

FESTERUS
TYPE: UNDEAD

At the edge of the woods, a decrepit wrought-iron gate has appeared, seemingly out of nowhere. There's nothing in sight beyond it, but a strange fellow in a filthy box office uniform quietly stands guard.

It seems you'll need to confront him to proceed, but do so at your own peril! He hurls enchanted tickets at you, and every few turns he unleashes a psychotic, ear-splitting laugh that can inflict frenzy, causing you to attack your own party members.

HP: 5,000 | **MP:** 230 | **WEAK:** fire, healing magic
IMMUNE: sleep, poison | **DROPS:** Old Ticket

OLD TICKET
ITEM057
INFO

A faded, dirty ticket, smudged with dirt and fingerprints. It looks faded and dingy, like it's from a long time ago. Hold it tightly and walk through the gate in the woods. But beware—this could be a one-way trip...

PINK WITCH CIRCUS

DUNGEON

One hundred years ago, a mysterious traveling circus set up outside Harbor City near the woods. It immediately captured the imagination of the town's children who were fascinated by the bright pink lights illuminating the night sky. But those who visited the circus never returned home. By the time their mothers and fathers realized they were missing, the circus had vanished without a trace... Why has it reappeared now?

EN025-026

COTTON CANDIES

RAZZ TYPE: ARTIFICIAL

Is it cotton candy or is it a ghost? It's both! This sweet specter can cause quite a fright, freezing you in place until your next turn. Spooky!

HP: 400 | **MP:** 0 | **WEAK:** water | **IMMUNE:** n/a

ROSIE TYPE: ARTIFICIAL

Similar to Razz, but it uses a variety of magic spells. They're very dangerous when encountered together! A blast from Penelope's water gun will render them useless for a couple rounds until they dry out and reform into clouds!

HP: 300 | **MP:** 200 | **WEAK:** water
IMMUNE: n/a

CIRCUS ENEMIES

CLOWN
TYPE: UNDEAD

These clowns run rampant, all dressed in the same colorful outfits and donning the same creepy face paint. Who were they before being employed by the circus? Nobody knows. They use powerful shadow magic and a variety of other weaker spells.

HP: 600 | **MP:** 400 | **WEAK:** silence
IMMUNE: n/a | **DROPS:** Joke Flower (rare)

MIME
TYPE: UNDEAD

Clowns use strong magic, but they're susceptible to the status ailment **silence**. Once afflicted, they transform into mimes. They can't use magic in this state, but their physical attacks increase. You can transform them back into clowns by curing their silent state.

HP: 575 | **MP:** 0 | **WEAK:** blind | **IMMUNE:** n/a | **DROPS:** Arcade Token (rare)

CIRCUS ENEMIES

JOLLY CHIMP AND SUNNY CHIMP   TYPE: ARTIFICIAL

These rusted, barely-functioning monkey toys are possessed by a vengeful spirit. They clap their cymbals at you, causing electric shock damage. They're weak to wind spells, which cause them to break apart, lowering their strength and defenses.

HP: 666 | **MP:** 0 | **WEAK:** wind | **IMMUNE:** n/a | **DROPS:** Pinwheel (rare)

SPOOKY CAT

GIMME SOMETHING TASTY!

A slinky black cat who roams the circus grounds, looking for **treats**. It will ask you for something tasty, so be a friend and toss it something scrumptious. It'll scamper off into the night, and something good might happen later.

HP: 1 | **MP:** 0 | **WEAK:** treats
IMMUNE: death

ITEM058-061

CIRCUS ITEMS

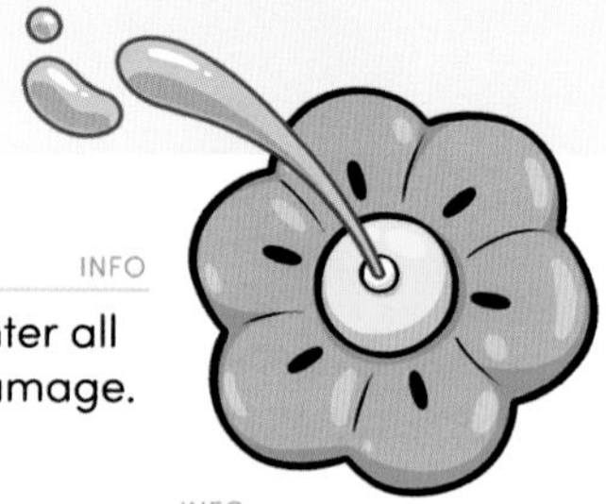

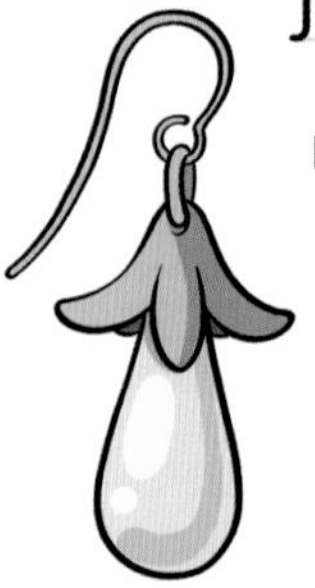

JOKE FLOWER

INFO

Equip this plastic accessory to counter all physical attacks with weak water damage.

LOST EARRING

INFO

A lovely earring, left behind by someone in a hurry. Raises your magic defense a bit.

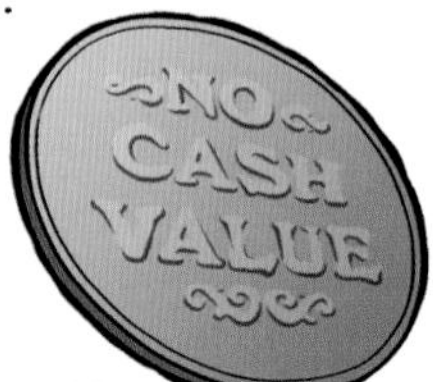
NO
CASH
VALUE

ARCADE TOKEN

INFO

An accessory that raises luck a little bit and increases money gained from battles.

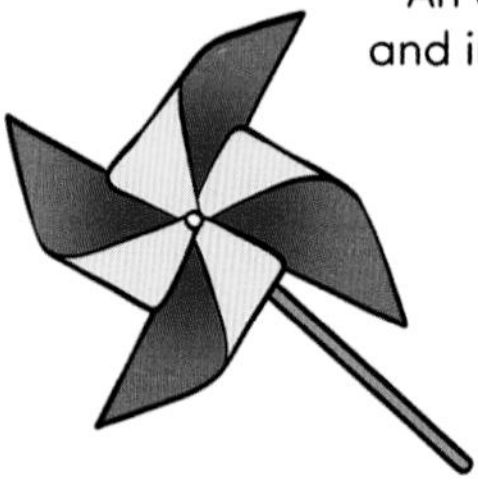

PINWHEEL

INFO

An accessory that raises resistance to wind-based spells while also increasing the potency of your own wind magic.

THE PINK WITCH

TYPE: HUMAN/UNDEAD

Once thought only a sinister fairy tale, it appears the Pink Witch is indeed real. Legend tells us of a beautiful but ruthless woman so eager to increase her own vitality that she turned to forbidden blood magic. Under the guise of a colorful circus, she moved from town to town, tempting the curious into her tent so that she might feast. They say she consumed so much blood that her own flesh became forever flushed, hence her moniker...

She can lance you with the end of her staff, causing you to bleed into her cup, which she can drink to replenish her own health. She also uses nearly every known spell and can pinpoint your exact weakness. You'll have to stay on your toes if you hope to lay her to rest for good!

HP: 9,500 | **MP:** 999 | **WEAK:** dark, holy | **IMMUNE:** silence, resistant to magic | **DROPS:** Pin Catalyst

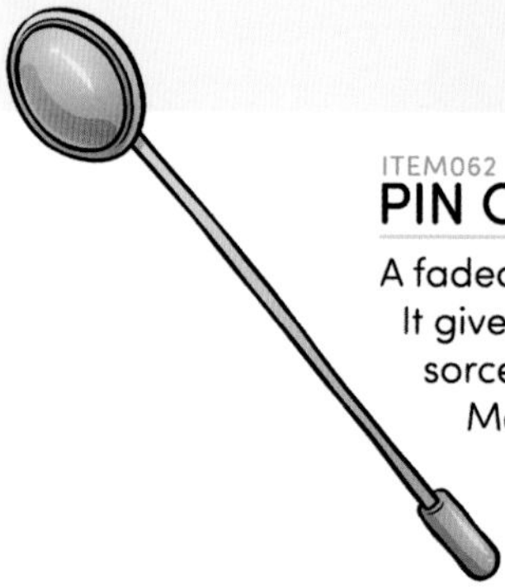

ITEM062

PIN CATALYST

INFO

A faded but still beautiful pin, used to secure a large hat. It gives off the eerie energy of a feared and respected sorceress. **Esther** snatches it and stuffs it in her bag. Maybe **Freja** can shed some light on its origin?

BOSS013

THE PINK WITCH

PINK WITCH

Ahhh, I can smell your **blood**... Be a dear and *give it to me!*

LEVEL 3 WEAPONS

CARNIVAL BAT
FINN

A colorful bat that packs a punch and very occasionally inflicts confusion.

ATK: 55 | **MAG:** 10 | **CRIT:** 30% | **ELEMENT:** none

TWIN GUPPIES
PENELOPE

These dual water pistols aren't the strongest, but they hit all enemies at once.

ATK: 20 | **MAG:** 39 | **CRIT:** 15% | **ELEMENT:** water

HAUNTED HOUSE
SOUND EFFECTS

SPOOKY BOOTLEG
CLAUDETTE

This rare recording contains strange songs that inflict a variety of different status ailments.

ATK: 35 | **MAG:** 55 | **CRIT:** 15% | **ELEMENT:** none

SLIDE WHISTLE
THEODORE

A fun novelty whistle that summons a carousel to trample enemies.

ATK: 33 | **MAG:** 50 | **CRIT:** 15% | **ELEMENT:** none

HOBBYHORSE
KNOX

A powerful equine weapon that sometimes inflicts slow.

ATK: 85 | **MAG:** 0 | **CRIT:** 15% | **ELEMENT:** none

Intermediate
Magic

INTERMEDIATE SPELLBOOK
ESTHER

A dense tome with difficult spells to master. Only for experienced witches who have an extensive knowledge of magic.

ATK: 0 | **MAG:** 80 | **CRIT:** n/a | **ELEMENT:** n/a

Ruby's House

DUNGEON

A cacophony of sounds coming from inside has drawn a crowd outside Theodore's house. His grandmother **Ruby** hasn't been seen in a few days. Is everything okay?

NPC007

THEO'S GRANDMA

RUBY   INFO

Since Theodore's parents are usually up north studying frozen plant life and microorganisms, his grandmother Ruby acts as sole caretaker. In her younger years she was the head cook for the army, and her impeccable skills in the kitchen are widely credited for invigorating the troops and winning the war (or at least that's how she tells the story). At any rate, her cooking talents are unmatched in all of Harbor City.

Recently, Ruby bought a peculiar **Dutch oven** at a garage sale that appears to be cursed by something wicked. Total catastrophe has broken out, and it threatens to spill out into the neighborhood! All of Ruby's delicious confections are coming to life and wreaking havoc. What on earth is going on?

KITCHEN ENEMIES

MUFFIN TOP
TYPE: PLANT

It's all that—multigrain, nonfat. I know you want a piece of that, but it's just here to kill you.

HP: 300 | **MP:** 0 | **WEAK:** fire | **IMMUNE:** n/a

MUFFIN BASE
TYPE: PLANT

The worst part of a muffin. Why does it even exist? Nobody likes the bottom of a muffin. Disgusting. High in fiber, though.

HP: 300 | **MP:** 0 | **WEAK:** water, ice | **IMMUNE:** n/a

SATSUMA TARTLET
TYPE: PLANT

A tangy treat? Think again! These disrespectful little tarts zoom around like tiny UFOs, flinging sour custard in your eyes, which can cause **darkness** and lower your accuracy. Very difficult to hit with standard attacks, unless you cast slow on them first.

HP: 290 | **MP:** 110 | **WEAK:** slow, magic, poison | **IMMUNE:** n/a

OOEY GOOEY KITCHEN RANGERS

This rambunctious group of desserts is anything but sweet! They've turned poor Ruby's home into a madhouse. You'll have to track them all down in different corners of the house and squash them if you want to restore peace to *Casa de Ruby*! If you're lucky, she might reward you with some (nondeadly) treats.

VISCOUNTESS JELLYROLL

TYPE: HYBRID

A dry and humorless Swiss roll. Her formidable strength, coupled with her high defense and HP, make her an imposing foe. Thankfully, she's susceptible to numerous status ailments.

HP: 10,000 | **MP:** 0 | **WEAK:** poison, slow, frenzy
IMMUNE: dark, silence

BARON VON SESAME

TYPE: HYBRID

He may have gotten a bit scrambled in the soft serve machine, but Baron von Sesame is no one to trifle with (yes, that is a pastry pun). He uses pesky confusion spells to make quick work of your party.

HP: 8,888 | **MP:** 888 | **WEAK:** dark
IMMUNE: confusion

PRINCESS PIÑA

TYPE: HYBRID

A little pineapple upside-down cake who would rather practice dance moves than fight. She's capable of using strong magic attacks, although it takes her a fairly long time to cast them.

HP: 7,500 | **MP:** 650 | **WEAK:** n/a | **IMMUNE:** silence

LORD MATCHA

TYPE: HYBRID

An enigmatic slice of matcha cake with a real bad attitude. He's not especially strong and he has no magical capabilites, but he's lightning fast and can attack multiple times per round. He can quickly whittle away your health if you're not careful, but thankfully he has low HP.

HP: 4,900 | **MP:** 0 | **WEAK:** magic | **IMMUNE:** slow

INQUISITOR FRAISE

TYPE: HYBRID

The leader of the Kitchen Rangers, he'll stop at nothing to lay waste to his enemies—and that means you! His all-around high stats make him a fearsome opponent indeed.

HP: 9,999 | **MP:** 0 | **WEAK:** poison
IMMUNE: dark, slow

KITCHEN RANGERS (FINAL FORM)

MEGATORTE
TYPE: HYBRID

Oh no! The Kitchen Rangers have morphed into their final form: a massive, sticky cake tower! Each layer can attack independently, so you'll have to rely on all your strengths to topple them once and for all.

HP: 3,000 per layer
MP: 200 per layer
WEAK: n/a | **IMMUNE:** n/a
DROPS: Decorative Catalyst

DECORATIVE CATALYST

INFO

A miniature, ornate spoon from Ruby's kitchen. It's imbued with the energy of a kindly beastmaster. Bring it to **Freja** to inspire an evolution in **Theodore**.

FREJA UNCHAINED

INFO

With all the catalysts collected, Freja's chains magically melt and disappear. She can feel the fog in her memory beginning to clear, though there is still much she can't recall. She understands that the items you've brought her, all apparently ordinary ephemera, were somehow imbued with energy from **dying beings from another world**, but the reasons why this dark energy found its way to Toro Island remain shrouded in mystery. Does it have anything to do with **Finn's accident**?

In the meantime, Freja will do what she can to help the party in their journey. With her strength restored, on rare occasions she'll appear in battle and attack baddies with her **golden spear**, instantly killing all enemies in the field. Perhaps she can put her arcane knowledge to use and craft some helpful new **artifacts** to ease your journey. She already has a few things in mind...

ITEM064
TRANSPORT CRYSTAL

INFO

With her newfound powers, Freja manifests these floating crystals across the island in places you've visited before, allowing you to quickly travel between them at will. Now you'll no longer have to backtrack to places you want to revisit! Very cool!

S.P.R.I.T.E.

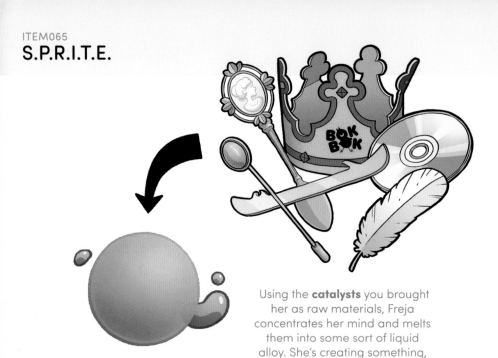

Using the **catalysts** you brought her as raw materials, Freja concentrates her mind and melts them into some sort of liquid alloy. She's creating something, but what on earth could it be?

S.P.R.I.T.E
Scanning **P**latform and **R**eporting **I**nterface for **T**racking **E**nemies

What's this? Freja has crafted a small handheld device that she can use to communicate with you! She calls it **SPRITE**, which stands for **S**canning **P**latform and **R**eporting **I**nterface for **T**racking **E**nemies. So how exactly does it work? Not even Freja knows, really! Somehow she's tapped into the currents of energy around the island and hears voices from all over, even if they're mostly just faint snippets. Now and then SPRITE will ring and Freja will have some news for you. Keep it handy, and always be sure to pick up when it rings!

FEVER MODE

Freja is able to extract the
latent energy of the catalysts
you brought her to bestow
new powers on your party.
You now have the ability to
harness **Fever Mode** in battle!
When a character lands hits
or takes damage, they'll fill
up their **Fever Meter**. When it's
maxed out, the character can
transform into a legendary
warrior with boosted stats
and a whole new set of spells
and techniques. Very useful!

FEARLESS TEMPLAR FINNEUS

INFO

In Fever Mode, Finn is able to call on the ancient powers of a legendary dedicated knight from another world who nobly fell in battle protecting his kingdom. He's granted a respectable boost in **strength** and **accuracy**, while a variety of potent light attacks become available. Additionally, any light-based attacks used against him are absorbed and do zero damage.

DOGGED HUNTER PENELOPE

INFO

In Fever Mode, Penelope's powerful arrows never miss and pierce through all armor defenses. She can also volley arrows into the sky to damage all enemies at once. Her **speed** doubles, meaning she can act two or three times before an enemy has a chance to move. In addition to doing heavy damage, she can target an enemy's specific stat (such as strength or defense) to permanently lower it.

VALLIANT CHAMPION KNOX

INFO

In Fever Mode, Knox gains astronomical **strength** and **defense**, becoming nearly invincible to physical attacks. He dons gold enchanted armor that was once worn by a mythical champion. It deflects most magic attacks, giving him the freedom to attack fearlessly with abandon. The only downside is that the armor is quite heavy, so he's even slower than usual.

CELESTIAL DIVINER CLAUDETTE

When entering Fever Mode, Claudette is overcome with rousing heavenly voices, and her songs are replaced with **mighty chants** that can greatly boost the party's stats. Her spells become more powerful, and she becomes totally invulnerable to all status ailments. Right before Fever Mode wears off, she calls on celestial holy rays to heavily damage all enemies.

CALAMITOUS WITCH ESTHER

INFO

In Fever Mode, Esther gains spells she barely understands and has tenuous control over. In addition to stronger elemental spells, she can use strange **Void Magic**, a terrifying form of sorcery that threatens to tear her apart if she uses it too much. No enemy in the game can withstand Void Magic, and she can easily obliterate even the strongest foes...but perhaps at a cost to her own sanity.

VIGILANT GEOMANCER THEODORE

INFO

In Fever Mode, Theodore gains huge **beastly gauntlets**, plus **powerful spells** that change depending on the environment. He draws on the energy of his surroundings to cast devastating spells that don't cost MP. He can also unleash a mighty roar, which instills fear and causes any beast-type enemy to immediately flee the battle area.

I'm hearing some odd chatter from deep in the **woods.** Wait until nightfall and go investigate!

Hemlock Wildwood

DUNGEON

INFO

The woods north of Harbor City are dark and dangerous! There are any number of gruesome rumors and ominous urban legends associated with the forest. Only the boldest dare venture into the shady thicket of the Hemlock Wildwood...and some never return...

EN039-040

FOREST ENEMIES

ENOKITAKE

TYPE: FUNGUS

He's definitely not a fun guy! These little shrooms use spore attacks to inflict poison, so keep an eye on your health! They tend to show up in clusters but luckily don't inflict too much physical damage.

HP: 500 | **MP:** 230
WEAK: fire, lightning
IMMUNE: poison

DEATH CAP

TYPE: FUNGUS

This worrisome mushroom moves incredibly slowly and only has one attack, but it's a doozy! It can inflict **instant fainting**, so make sure to stock up on healing items!

HP: 490 | **MP:** 110 | **WEAK:** fire | **IMMUNE:** poison

FOREST ENEMIES

BIG CHAMP
TYPE: FUNGUS

A lumbering, meaty mushroom who can wipe out your whole party in a single blow if you're not properly leveled. It might be best to run away from these unless you're feeling exceptionally lucky! If you do manage to take one down, they give lots of EXP and money!

HP: 8,000 | **MP:** 340
WEAK: fire, sometimes sleep
IMMUNE: poison

FOX WITH A KNIFE
TYPE: BEAST

It's a fox with a knife.

HP: 700 | **MP:** 0 | **WEAK:** lightning | **IMMUNE:** n/a

MUSHROOM BOY

INFO

A little boy who used to be human before weird things started happening on the island and he mutated into a mushroom. He doesn't seem too concerned by his new form, though! The creatures in the woods don't seem to bother with him, and he minds his own business. He's quite friendly and will happily sell you **mushrooms**. He also tells you that he was separated from his sister, whom he last saw on the beach. If you see her, tell her that her brother says hi!

ITEM066-069
MUSHROOMS, ETC.

MUSHROOM INFO

A plain mushroom. Doesn't seem useful on its own, but you can turn it into a gummy!

POISON MUSHROOM INFO

Careful! It's poisonous! It can be turned into a very gross-tasting gummy, if you want!

MUSTY GUMMY INFO

A distinctly...earthy flavored gummy made from mushrooms. Eat it to double your physical attack power for a few turns.

POISON GUMMY INFO

A bitter gummy made from poison mushrooms. Can be used on enemies to inflict **poison**, or you can eat it yourself to boost resistance to all status ailments.

RAINDEER TYPE: BEAST

Graceful yet deadly, this creature patrols the very darkest part of the woods. Though it appears to be an enormous deer, in reality it's something else, something old and evil. Why it's donned this antlered disguise is any-body's guess, but this much is apparent: it will stop at nothing to trample the life out of you. In battle, it uses swift kicks to inflict damage, and it can summon toxic rain that will halve one random stat for a few turns, such as strength, magic, or speed.

HP: 12,000 | **MP:** 590
WEAK: light **IMMUNE:** n/a
DROPS: Graveyard Key

ITEM070
GRAVEYARD KEY   INFO

A decrepit skeletal hand. The pointer finger has been carved into the shape of a key. Who did this hand belong to? It's better not to think about it

DESOLATE GRAVEYARD

DUNGEON

In the woods there's an untended cemetary surrounded by a tall, crumbling stone wall covered in moss. It looks like nobody's been there in a long time. The **skeletal key** you just picked up opens the creaky front gate. What sort of horrors await you there?

EN043-044
GRAVEYARD ENEMIES

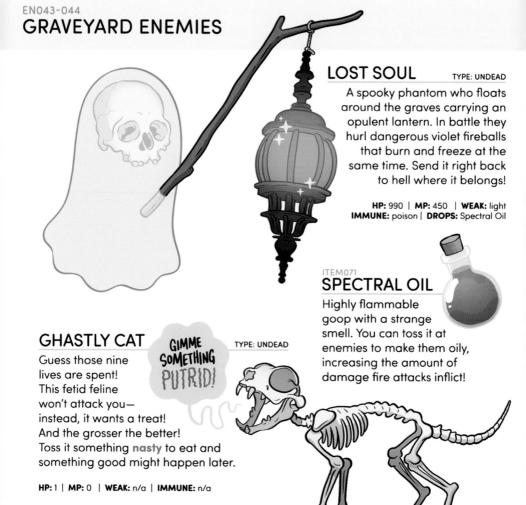

LOST SOUL   TYPE: UNDEAD

A spooky phantom who floats around the graves carrying an opulent lantern. In battle they hurl dangerous violet fireballs that burn and freeze at the same time. Send it right back to hell where it belongs!

HP: 990 | **MP:** 450 | **WEAK:** light
IMMUNE: poison | **DROPS:** Spectral Oil

ITEM071
SPECTRAL OIL

Highly flammable goop with a strange smell. You can toss it at enemies to make them oily, increasing the amount of damage fire attacks inflict!

GHASTLY CAT   TYPE: UNDEAD

GIMME SOMETHING PUTRID!

Guess those nine lives are spent! This fetid feline won't attack you—instead, it wants a treat! And the grosser the better! Toss it something **nasty** to eat and something good might happen later.

HP: 1 | **MP:** 0 | **WEAK:** n/a | **IMMUNE:** n/a

CORVIDS

TYPE: UNDEAD

Is it a boss or a minigame? Yes! In the graveyard, many of the tombstones have a creepy crow perched atop them—but only one is the real boss. Attack the wrong one, and you'll be forced to battle a dangerous flock of crows. Choose correctly, and Corvid will burst into blue flames. After a few rounds of battle, he'll fly off and find a new perch and you'll have to seek him out again. Corvid attacks with piercing strikes and can also let loose an earsplitting cry that reduces your whole party's MP to zero.

HP: 12,000
MP: 300
WEAK: n/a
IMMUNE: n/a

ITEM072
BLOODY KEY CARD

INFO

The graveyard is quiet—*too* quiet. Whatever was happening here, it's over now. But there's a freshly exhumed grave with no body in sight. What sort of nefarious plot have you stumbled onto? There is but a single clue: a **key card** on the ground, apparently abandoned during a hasty exit. It's splattered with blood, making it difficult to read, but perhaps it will still prove useful. There's not much to go off, but the logo features an icon of a **lighthouse**... Hey, isn't there a lighthouse on the beach? And come to think of it, you've never actually seen it lit up at night...

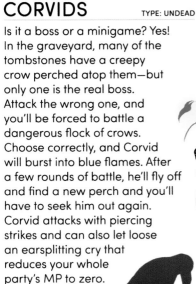

OLD LIGHTHOUSE

DUNGEON

On a secluded stretch of the beach, there's what seems to be a decommissioned lighthouse. Once inside, you see that's not the case at all. Inside the tower is empty, save for a single **terminal** in the center of the room, asking for your credentials...

BEA⬤CON
LABORATORIES

DUNGEON

Using the **key card** you found in the graveyard causes the ground to groan and start moving. This isn't a lighthouse at all—it's an enormous elevator. It takes you deep underground to a clandestine facility called Beacon Laboratories.
How has this place operated in secret for so long? What's going on here?

EN045
LABORATORY ENEMIES

ZOMBIE
TYPE: UNDEAD

The dead have risen! Why is this lab full of reanimated corpses? What kind of wicked scheme have you uncovered here?

In addition to doing heavy physical damage, zombies can lunge forward and bite you, turning you into a zombie, too! If this happens, your health will slowly deplete and you'll become impervious to healing spells and items. Instead, you'll have to use an item that normally revives a fallen party member!

HP: 1 | **MP:** 0 | **WEAK:** n/a | **IMMUNE:** n/a

BOSS017-018

DR. NOGUCHI AND CALLIOPE

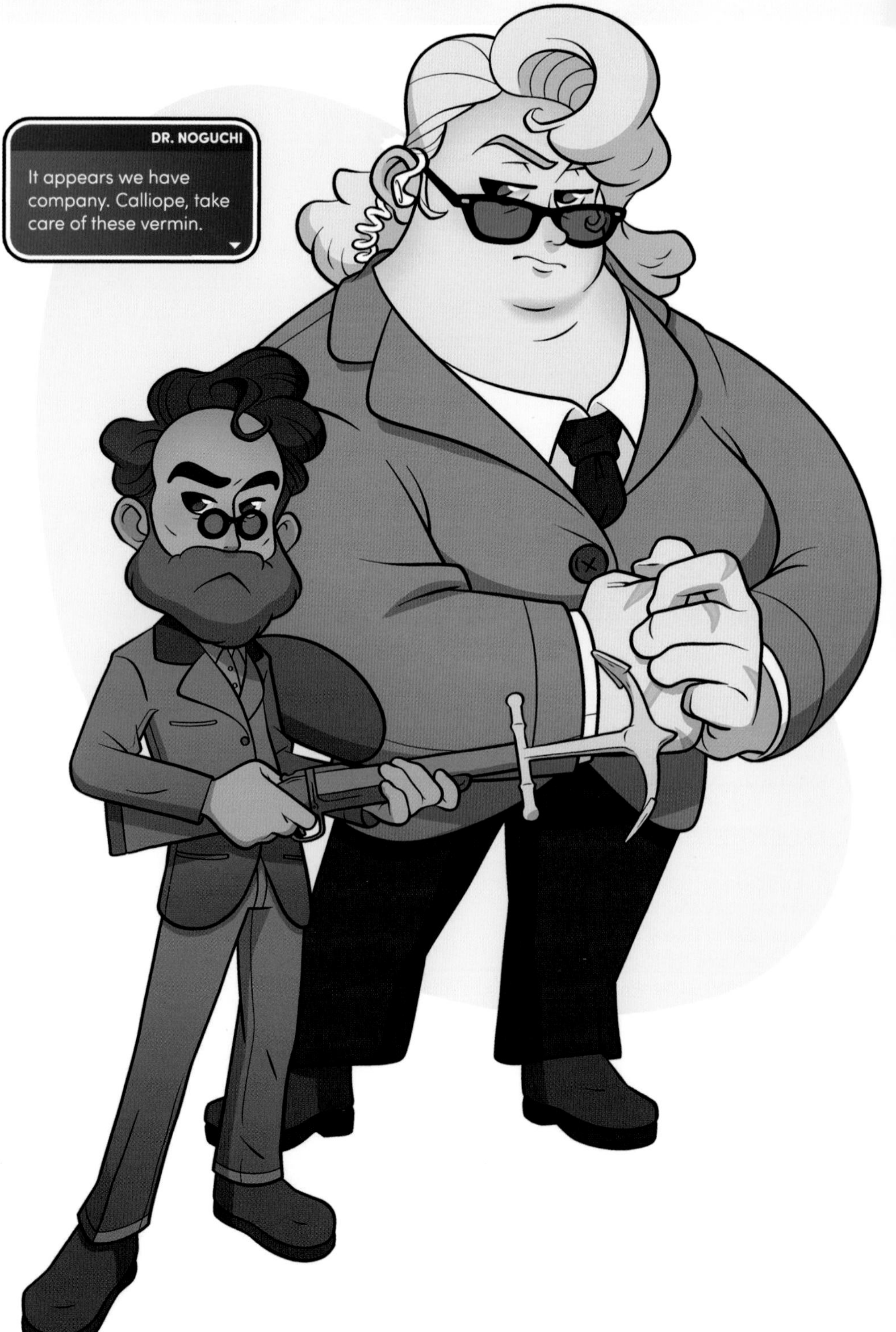
DR. NOGUCHI
It appears we have company. Calliope, take care of these vermin.

DR. NOGUCHI
TYPE: HUMAN

Dr. Nikolai Noguchi is a brilliant and ambitious biologist. His scientific advances have made him rich and respected, but several years ago, after the sudden death of his wife, he disappeared from public view entirely, practically overnight. What has he been studying while holed up underground for so long?

Noguchi primarily relies on his bodyguard, Calliope, to protect him in battle, and doesn't directly attack on his own. However, he'll periodically launch his anchor gun at a party member, removing them from battle for a single turn.

HP: 11,500 | **MP:** 0 | **WEAK:** poison, fire | **IMMUNE:** n/a

CALLIOPE
TYPE: HUMAN

Calliope is Dr. Noguchi's bodyguard, always at his side to deal with whatever riffraff gets in his way. She can clobber you with heavy punches, and her incredibly high HP and defense make her a difficult foe to vanquish. She's weak to magic, though, so it's best to rely on your most powerful spells.

HP: 16,000 | **MP:** 0 | **WEAK:** magic | **IMMUNE:** n/a | **DROPS:** Lab Key

ITEM073
LAB KEY
INFO

A plain key with a code written on the keychain. There's a locked door at the end of a a hallway with a keypad. It couldn't hurt to try it out...but are you prepared for what you might find?

???

TYPE: ???

A grotesque specimen found at **Starfish Beach** after a mysterious calamity.
Upon seeing it, Finn begins to recall something, but collapses before he can
make sense of the memory. How did this appendage end up here in a lab?
Does it somehow seem...alive? Something has reanimated it and now it
radiates a bizarre energy, emitting dangerous beams when attacked.
It seems there's no choice but to destroy it.

HP: 13,400 | **MP:** 520 | **WEAK:** n/a | **IMMUNE:** n/a | **DROPS:** Noguchi's Journal

NOGUCHI'S JOURNAL

Press ✗ to open

Wednesday

I've made an odd discovery. The morning after we recorded the anomaly, one of my assistants found this severed arm washed up on the shore near the lighthouse. Upon bringing it to the lab, I discovered that the cells still seem to be active. Or rather, they've been reactivated by something I can't detect. I have to run some more tests to figure out what's going on, but so far the arm shows no sign of decomposition or necrosis. In fact, when I sliced off a piece of the arm, it had healed within a few hours. I've taken a few more samples, as well as a few vials of blood.

I have an idea. I'll need some more supplies, however...

I know you've got a lot on your plate, but someone dialed in requesting your assistance!

...I'm actually not sure how they did that...

CAMP CONIFER

DUNGEON

INFO

For countless decades, Hemlock Wildwood has been a dreary and dangerous tangle of shadowy trees, full of mysterious monsters. Now, with the evil forces eliminated by your party, the woods are finally transforming for the better. Sunlight is breaking through the canopy and friendly animals are at last returning to the woods.

Word travels fast! **Ranger Bex** wants to open a new **summer camp**, but the forest isn't quite safe yet! There are many strange beasts still roaming about, snapping up woodland creatures and giving Bex trouble. There's a small abandoned farm deep in the forest that would make the perfect spot for her summer camp—help clear out Hemlock Wildwood for good and you'll be handsomely rewarded. This is an **optional side quest**, but it could be worth your while!

NPC009
CAMP COUNSELOR

An accomplished naturalist, Bex has been dying to explore Hemlock Wildwood for ages, but the nefarious creatures that roamed the forest kept her away. Now that the Pink Witch has been eliminated, Bex can finally get to work! She's decided to open a summer camp where kids can learn to be buff and outdoorsy like her, but there's still a lot of work to do before the grand opening. The forest isn't totally clear of monsters yet, and she needs them taken care of before she can start enrolling campers. If you help out and make sure the woods are safe, she'll definitely reward you!

Once you ensure that the woods are safe for Bex to open up camp, you can recruit certain NPCs you've met to sign up as camp counselors, and Bex will pay you commission at regular intervals! It's not a pyramid scheme; it's multilevel marketing. Please learn the difference!

CHICKENS

CHICKLET
TYPE: BEAST

A chunky little chicken who bops around the woods looking for things to gnaw on. Fairly weak but often found in clusters. When it's low on HP, it shrieks for backup.

HP: 300 | **MP:** 0 | **WEAK:** n/a | **IMMUNE:** n/a

SPICY CHICKLET
TYPE: BEAST

This chicklet has a temper! Much stronger than ordinary chicklets, it attacks with dangerous fire breath that can quickly roast your party.

HP: 300 | **MP:** 220 | **WEAK:** ice, water
IMMUNE: fire, dark, slow

SNOWY CHICKLET
TYPE: BEAST

A frozen chicklet who fell asleep during a blizzard. Now it's covered in a thick layer of permafost that acts as dense armor. You'll have to melt it if you want to do any serious damage!

HP: 300 | **MP:** 250 | **WEAK:** fire | **IMMUNE:** ice, sleep

FLASH CHICKLET

TYPE: BEAST

A lightning-quick chicklet who ate some strange berries in the forest. Now it zips around, unable to focus, crashing into your party with electrified jolts.

HP: 300 | **MP:** 130 | **WEAK:** poison
IMMUNE: lightning, wind

SHADOW CHICKLET

TYPE: BEAST

A normal chicklet who found a mysterious hat somewhere in the woods. Now it can cast a bunch of different spells and cause status ailments in your group. Very annoying!

HP: 500 | **MP:** 400 | **WEAK:** light
IMMUNE: shadow, poison

CHICKLET ASCENDANT

TYPE: BEAST

A chicklet who ate the soul of another chicklet, gaining its powers and abilities. It is able to strike with many different elemental spells, including holy attacks. Quite dangerous, so stay vigilant!

HP: 950 | **MP:** 500 | **WEAK:** shadow | **IMMUNE:** light

FOUL ASSASSIN

HEN OF THE WOODS
TYPE: HYBRID

The Hen of the Woods was once a cruel assassin with untold kills. After countless years of clandestine operations, she abruptly retired, settling down on a small ranch to raise chickens. Legend says her chickens were the meanest in all the land, and every egg they laid was green and rotten. Over the years, the assassin began to resemble her chickens more and more, until she finally died at the age of 108. By the time her body was discovered, she was nothing but bones, picked clean by her beloved, evil chickens.

Now, some sinister force has revived her as a bizarre human/chicken hybrid. Meaner than ever and twice as deadly, she attacks with her double swords, easily slicing your health away. At half health, she applies poison to her blades, so keep your wits about you!

HP: 15,550 | **MP:** 0 | **WEAK:** wind, slow | **IMMUNE:** dark | **DROPS:** Small Pouch

In the Hen's home, there's a wooden box with three sliding lids. When you open one, the other two lock permanently. There's a handy **new accessory** in each compartment, but you may only choose one! Decide wisely!

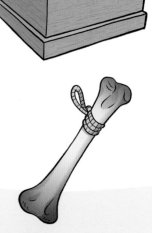

ITEM075A
GRIMY TUFT INFO
An oily, tattered feather plucked from a malicious chicken. Increases all **magic attacks** by 50%. Tremendous!

ITEM075B
FOUL CLAW INFO
A smelly, rigid chicken claw from a ferocious bird. Increases all **physical attacks** by 50%. Marvelous!

ITEM075C
FADED BONE INFO
An old bone picked clean of meat. Boosts both **physical and magic defense** by a decent 25%. Astonishing!

SMALL POUCH

INFO

A tiny, worn pouch made of chicken skin. It's gross, but it's useful! Now every party member can equip an **additional accessory** in battle!

I'm faintly sensing someone with the same **Fever Mode** power as you up north in the mountains... Could it be a new **ally**?

CONDEMNED QUARTZ MINES

DUNGEON

INFO

There are dangerous mines at the base of the Cobblerock Mountains. For many decades their depths were excavated for rare green quartz, allowing Harbor City to rapidly expand in size and wealth. Eventually the miners drilled too deep, flooding most parts of the cave system and causing the total closure of the mines altogether. But Freja has sensed a powerful presence in the supposedly abandoned mines. Who has breached the barricades, and what are they doing there?

EN047
MINE ENEMIES

CRYSTALOISE   TYPE: BEAST

A slow-moving but hardy turtle lookin' for some fingies to chomp. Physical attacks do limited damage, and while it is weak to magic, it'll store energy from magical attacks in its crystal shell, eventually unleashing a devastating spell that wallops your whole party.

HP: 999 | **MP:** 300 | **WEAK:** dark, magic
IMMUNE: slow, poison | **DROPS:** Prasiolite Chunk

ITEM076
PRASIOLITE CHUNK

INFO

A nugget of green quartz, radiating with energy. Perhaps it can be used to make weapons?

TROLL   TYPE: BEAST

A gnarled creature who meanders the mines looking for shiny trinkets left behind by humans. It wields a crooked staff topped with a skull that mutters incantations that block your party from casting any spells, both offensive and curative. Eliminate the skull quickly or you might find yourself in a real pickle!

HP: 400 (skull) 750 (troll) | **MP:** 340
WEAK: wind | **IMMUNE:** frenzy

CRYSTAL SLIME   TYPE: SLIME

This is definitely *not* a red palette swap of the Cave Slimes from earlier but with higher HP and the ability to use fire spells. Look, disc space is limited. Do you have any idea how hard it is to keep coming up with new enemy designs? Sometimes people need a break. How dare you criticize someone else for reusing a few assets! *How dare you.*

HP: 8,000 | **MP:** 340 | **WEAK:** fire | **IMMUNE:** poison

AMELIA (FEVER MODE)

AMELIA

You don't even know who you are, Finn... You don't know *anything*.

AMELIA

You can't stand in the way of what's about to happen....*NOW DIE!*

EXECUTIONER AMELIA

TYPE: HUMAN

The power Freja sensed in the mines was no ally; it was **Amelia**—and somehow she's been granted the power of **Fever Mode**, too. Who bestowed this power to her, and where exactly did it come from in the first place? She's been here in the mines, using the crystals to gather energy from the earth, growing even more powerful.

Her mallet has been replaced with an enormous hammer that crackles with electricity. Brace yourself for a difficult fight, because Amelia won't go down easy.

HP: 22,222 | **MP:** 222 | **WEAK:** n/a | **IMMUNE:** poison, dark, silence, sleep | **DROPS:** Amelia's Amulet

AMELIA (FINAL FORM)

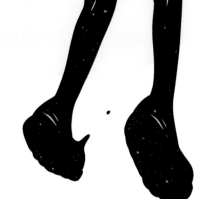

VANAGLORIA   TYPE: COSMIC

Losing the battle, Amelia calls on some dreadful, otherwordly force. A giant eye opens on her forehead, revealing all possible outcomes of the battle. Seeing that she fails no matter what, she loses whatever shred of humanity was left in her, transforming into **Vanagloria**. If she can't beat you in battle, she'll die trying.

HP: 21,212 | **MP:** 212 | **WEAK:** light
IMMUNE: poison, silence, sleep | **DROPS:** Black Pearl

ITEM077
AMELIA'S AMULET   INFO

Amelia's onyx amulet. It appears to have been stabbed, and as a result, it no longer opens. You can equip it as an accessory to increase dark magic resistance.

ITEM078
BLACK PEARL   INFO

A large, heavy pearl, dark as midnight. It emanates a sinister aura and makes you feel sick to your stomach. Amelia had somehow managed to use it as a catalyst, but in the end, it destroyed her.

ITEM079
PINK PEARL   INFO

If you give the black pearl to Freja, she is able to purify it. This shiny pink pearl can be used on any party member to permanently raise each of their stats by 3. Not bad!

Prasiolite Chunks can be used to upgrade certain weaker weapons into new magical gear, but the previous weapon will be lost. These crystals can also be used to craft useful items and accessories!

CRYSTAL BAT   FINN

A craggy bat with good physical damage that also delivers minor non-elemental magic damage

ATK: 75 | **MAG:** 15 | **CRIT:** 40%
ELEMENT: none

CRYSTAL STICK   KNOX

This hockey stick offers a slight physical upgrade while also improving magic defense and critical chance a little bit.

ATK: 95 | **MAG:** 0 | **CRIT:** 20%
ELEMENT: none

CRYSTAL OCARINA   THEODORE

An elegant instrument that summons a swarm of crystal spiders to overwhelm enemies and sometimes freeze them in place.

ATK: 45 | **MAG:** 60 | **CRIT:** 25%
ELEMENT: ice

CRYSTAL PENDANT   ANYONE

A chunky accessory that improves the potency of all spells. Incredibly powerful when paired with a magic tome!

CRYSTAL DUST   PENELOPE

Add this useful powder to the tank of any water gun to add moderate magic damage to physical attacks for five turns.

HONEY MERCHANT

BEEKEEPER BLYTHE INFO

Your party barely has time to process what happened in the mines before you're thrust into another sticky situation. On the way out of the quarry, a frantic woman stumbles past, chasing after a swarm of bees, yelling for help. Follow her and find out what's going on!

Blythe is a kindly but odd woman who cares about little else than her beloved bees. Their honey is known far and wide for being the best around. She'll gladly sell you a jar or two if you help her out with something.

Lately, a nearby farm has been placing huge orders of honey, and Blythe hasn't been able to keep up with production and deliveries at the same time. She's had to get more bees, and the orders are piling up. Her hives are a mess, and she needs your assistance. If you can deliver the next order of honey to **Charmroot Farms** for her, it'll take some pressure off and she can hopefully get her business in order.

ITEM080
THISTLE HONEY INFO

A rich and delicious honey but quite expensive. Throw it at enemies to inflict **slow**.

ITEM081
ROYAL JELLY INFO

Blythe's most luxurious honey and the specific type Charmroot Farms has been ordering. Inflicts both **slow** and **frenzy** on enemies, but you shouldn't use it up or you'll have to buy more to deliver! Best to just hold on to it for now.

CHARMROOT FARMS

DUNGEON

Charmroot Farms is the largest provider of fruits and vegetables around, supplying produce to all the islands in Saltbrine Archipelago and even servicing parts of the mainland. Well, until recently, that is...

After a sudden round of canceled orders, the farm closed entirely and stopped responding to all queries from outsiders. Why has the farm suddenly gone dark? Why're the workers so protective of the **Great Barn**...?

EN050

FARM ENEMIES

DRONE   TYPE: HUMAN/BUG

Something is wrong with the workers at Charmroot Farms! These peculiar individuals buzz around the pasture in clumsy homemade costumes. Do they think that they're bees?

These drones won't respond to your inquiries, but they will attack you on sight if you venture too close to the big red barn in the middle of the compound. They tend to attack in groups and can be very dangerous, but throwing honey at them will cause **slow** and also distract them for a few rounds.

HP: 960 | **MP:** 340 | **WEAK:** wind, honey
IMMUNE: dark, poison

CURSED SCARECROW

TYPE: PLANT

INFO

An optional boss perched out in a distant field, he spews toxic gas that slowly depletes the HP of anyone who comes too close. This is different from poison—you can't cure it during battle, so make sure your HP doesn't get too low. The noxious gas, coupled with his surprisingly high HP, makes him a serious threat. Keep your distance unless you've got a death wish! He's a tough foe... but he's highly flammable.

HP: 25,000 | **MP:** 550 | **WEAK:** fire
IMMUNE: poison, sleep, slow
DROPS: Cursed Button

NPC011

HAPPY SCARECROW

INFO

Once defeated, the **Cursed Scarecrow** transforms into a **Happy Scarecrow**. If you check back every so often, he'll tell you new jokes that he's learned. He knows over 100! He's outstanding in his field.

ITEM082
CURSED BUTTON

INFO

A powerful artifact with a curious hex attached to it. Equip it as an accessory to raise all of your stats by 10, but your HP will also slowly deplete while you wear it!

SCIENCE QUIZ!

NAOMI THE CHEMIST
TYPE: ???

Naomi is the brilliant biochemical engineer who ensures the produce leaving the farm is packed full of vitamins and is almost alarmingly huge. But lately, her studies seem to have shifted elsewhere. She invented the **honeychoke**, and she seems to be hard at work using Blythe's luscious honey in other strange projects. And say, how the heck did she manage to grow wings?

Naomi guards the Great Barn, so you'll have to get past her if you want to investigate what's happening inside. You can challenge Naomi to a test of knowledge where she'll quiz you on science facts. If you answer them all correctly, she'll step aside. If you miss one, you'll have to fight her. She's not terribly tough, but she can fly, making it tough to land hits!

HP: 13,500 | **MP:** 0 | **WEAK:** projectiles | **IMMUNE:** sleep

MISS MELLONA

Turns out there wasn't anything nefarious happening in the Great Barn after all! Just the kindly **Miss Mellona**, owner, CEO, and prime shareholder of Charmroot Farms, dutifully overseeing production of their newest product—the **honeychoke!** It's a delicious honey-infused artichoke. How exciting!

In fact, she's offering you a **job** here on the farm! Stay and become one of her faithful employees! There's no pay and you can never go home, but you get free room and board! That's not nothing! If you accept, the game will end, and you'll spend the rest of your days blissfully buzzing around, eating nothing but honeychokes!

Accept
Decline

MISS MELLONA (TRUE FORM)

INSECT QUEEN

TYPE: HUMAN/BUG

As if you ever had a choice to leave! Mellona has been running Charmroot Farms for years, but the more her riches grew, the greedier she became. Her desire for power led her to genetically modify a poisonous artichoke by infusing it with a mind controlling serum that turns normal humans into mindless drones. But the serum was bitter, and Mellona needed something sweet to mask the taste. That explains why the farm has been buying up all the honey!

Mellona won't directly attack in battle; rather she'll take over the minds of two party members each turn, utilizing their most potent attacks against the rest of the party.

HP: 13,500 | **MP:** 0
WEAK: fire, wind
IMMUNE: n/a

MISS MELLONA (FINAL FORM)

AVARITIA

TYPE: COSMIC

Once vanquished, Mellona collapses, only to shed her human form and rise again as the being known as Avaritia, a creature devoid of all rational thought beyond the desire to destroy. She resembles the being Amelia transformed into... Why are people mutating into these horrific monsters?

Avaritia slithers around, whipping you with her huge tail. She can latch onto you, siphoning off your health to replenish her own. She's extremely weak to light and lightning, so make sure to use some spells and she should go down for good. Stay vigilant!

HP: 11,000 | **MP:** 680
WEAK: light, lightning
IMMUNE: poison

TEA MERCHANT

TEAMASTER KIERAN
INFO

Once you help Blythe with her errands at Charmroot Farms, she'll notify you that her friend Kieran is having similar troubles with their tea business. Kieran can be found at the base of the mountains, which isn't too far away!

Teamaster Kieran has but one mission in life: to craft the most delicate, balanced cup of tea ever brewed! They spend their days in the Mellowrift Teafields, tirelessly searching for the most tender leaves. They've heard rumors of a new shrub at the highest peak, but it's swarming with monsters. There are also reports of a hulking beast tearing up tea plants and causing general havoc. Perhaps if you clear the way for Kieran, they'll brew you something special?

ITEM083
SIMPLE TEACUP
INFO

A plain but elegant teacup. Though it doesn't appear particularly valuable, it brews extremely powerful tea. With the right ingredients, Teamaster Kieran can create useful one-time tonics to use in battle. Keep an eye out on the mountain for colorful sprigs so you can make some tasty teas in the future!

ITEM084-087
TEA LEAVES
INFO

A myriad of tea plants can be found on the mountain, and they all do different things! Sweetly fragrant **green tea** is used in battle to increase the potency of all healing magic. Bitter, unctuous **black tea** can be used in battle to increase magic damage dealt. Fancy **pink tea** increases the party's resistance to status ailments and blesses them. Moonbuds make ghost tea, allowing a single party member to be auto-raised if they faint.

MELLOWRIFT TEAFIELD

DUNGEON

Mellowrift Teafield sits atop steep cliffs in the Cobblerock Mountains, where the rarest teas grow. Only the most capable farmers dare to hike the dangerous ridges to harvest the coveted leaves. Menacing enemies prowl these precipitous crags, and the high winds make these teafields quite perilous!

EN051-052
GNOMES

CRABBY GNOMEWIFE
TYPE: BEAST

These pint-sized witches are proficient in **Acorn Augury**, a mysterious and ancient magic that's as befuddling as it is deadly. In addition to potent earth-based spells, they can transform you into an acorn, rendering you useless for a couple turns.

HP: 1,000 | **MP:** 500 | **WEAK:** n/a | **IMMUNE:** silence

IRRITABLE GNOME
TYPE: BEAST

Don't be fooled by these gremlins' cute and cuddly appearance—they'll chop you to bits and cook you up to feed to their grubby little kids. Highly territorial, they tend to attack in groups and overwhelm your party with quick whacks from their razor-sharp dual axes.

HP: 1,000 | **MP:** 0 | **WEAK:** n/a | **IMMUNE:** dark

CRACKPOT TYPE: HYBRID

A curious humanoid teapot that hurls clumps of wet tea leaves at your party. Once every few turns it blasts a cloud of steam across the whole battlefield, inducing lethargy and inflicting **slow**. If you cast fire spells on it, Crackpot will transform into a more powerful version of itself, becoming a much more difficult foe but granting higher experience points once defeated.

HP: 1,400 | **MP:** 90 | **WEAK:** fire
IMMUNE: slow, poison

ROYAL CRACKPOT TYPE: HYBRID

Someone's feeling a little hot under the collar! These guys move quicker and hit harder, and can blast your whole team with advanced fire magic. They're extremely dangerous, even if you're overleveled, so be careful! You can transform them back into regular Crackpots with water if you're feeling overwhelmed. But if you're feeling bold, you'll earn triple experience at the end of the battle.

HP: 7,777 | **MP:** 777 | **WEAK:** water
IMMUNE: slow, poison

WRATHFUL TEAGOLEM

TYPE: UNDEAD/COSMIC

A hulking beast created from thick mud and rotten tea leaves, brought to life with forbidden magic. It's been rampaging across the teafields, destroying equipment and killing anyone in its path. What created this monstrosity? Although its attacks are fairly straighforward, it moves surprisingly quickly for such a lumbering giant, and it can pummel your whole party with earth-shaking ground strikes. Keep an eye on your HP or you'll meet an early grave!

HP: 22,000 | **MP:** 0 | **WEAK:** light, healing magic | **IMMUNE:** poison, dark, zombie, death

Things are getting worse on the island. I need some **new supplies** if we're going to figure out what's causing all this chaos!

Whatever oppressive force has been transforming people on the island, it seems to be getting more dire. What started on the beach has spread to the whole island, and Freja can't seem to pinpoint the cause. She thinks she can upgrade the **SPRITE system** to filter out the noise and hone in on the source of the chaos, but she needs more materials. There's a salvage scrapper near Harbor City who might be able to help...

NPC014

SALVAGE MECHANIC

EDDY
INFO

Eddy used to work as a mechanic on a ship but couldn't get over the seasickness. After losing an eye in an unfortunate incident involving a flock of agitated seagulls, he retired from ship life. Now he lives by the seashore, collecting shells and artifacts to repair and sell. He always talks about returning to a life on the open seas, but while he won't admit it, he's really a landlubber at heart. He'll sell you any number of strange contraptions, though nearly all of them are useless. Recently he's noticed a **strange whirlpool** offshore. It's always in the same spot and never disappears. If you can bring him a **diving helmet**, he'll repair it, and you can explore the vortex. Maybe you can find something to help Freja!

EN055

NEPTUNE
INFO

Neptune is Eddy's cat and constant companion. Eddy saved him from a seagull attack and they've been best friends ever since. He's curious and adventurous, and won't sit still long enough for you to pet him. He'll engage in playful battle with you, though he's far too quick for you to land a hit. But if you give him something slimy, something good might happen later...

HP: 1 | **MP:** 1 | **WEAK:** n/a | **IMMUNE:** n/a

Jump in?

Yes
No

derelict warplanes

DUNGEON

INFO

Decades ago, during a misguided war, dozens of bombers were shot out of the sky and sunk to the bottom of the ocean, seemingly lost forever. For some reason, these undersea wrecks have all suddenly begun emitting a **curious frequency.** And somewhere in the wreckage, a peculiar energy has appeared. Could this be the cause of the whirlpool? Be careful as you investigate from wreckage to wreckage. Many of the planes have become home to sinister creatures, and danger lurks around every sodden corner!

OCEAN ENEMIES

CLOWNFISH   TYPE: BEAST

These little fish aren't too dangerous on their own, but they're encountered in schools of up to nine, so they can quickly overwhelm you if you're caught off guard. They hover around anemones who protect them from attacks, so take care of those first. Then a strong spell that targets multiple foes at once will make quick work of them.

HP: 450 | **MP:** 100 | **WEAK:** fire
IMMUNE: water | **DROPS:** Raw Coral

ANEMONE   TYPE: PLANT

An enemy anemone! These strange polyps aren't at all aggressive unless a clownfish is attacked while they're alive. If that occurs, the anemone will release a toxic cloud across your party that causes **poison, silence,** and **dark.** Make sure it's eliminated before you take on any pesky fish!

HP: 950 | **MP:** 0 | **WEAK:** fire | **IMMUNE:** poison, water | **DROPS:** Raw Coral

UNDEAD PILOT
TYPE: HUMAN/UNDEAD

A waterlogged aviator, cursed to roam the sea floor for eternity. These lumbering soldiers attack with slow but powerful punches, and every few turns they launch a torpedo that reduces your entire party's HP to zero. Make sure to heal quickly, or you'll be fish food!

HP: 1,620 | **MP:** 0 | **WEAK:** ice
IMMUNE: n/a | **DROPS:** Raw Coral

ITEM088
RAW CORAL
INFO

A hard chunk of shiny coral, found in the deepest depths of the sea. It's dropped by most enemies in the area, and it can be used to make lots of different useful accessories!

BOSS028

CARNAL SIREN

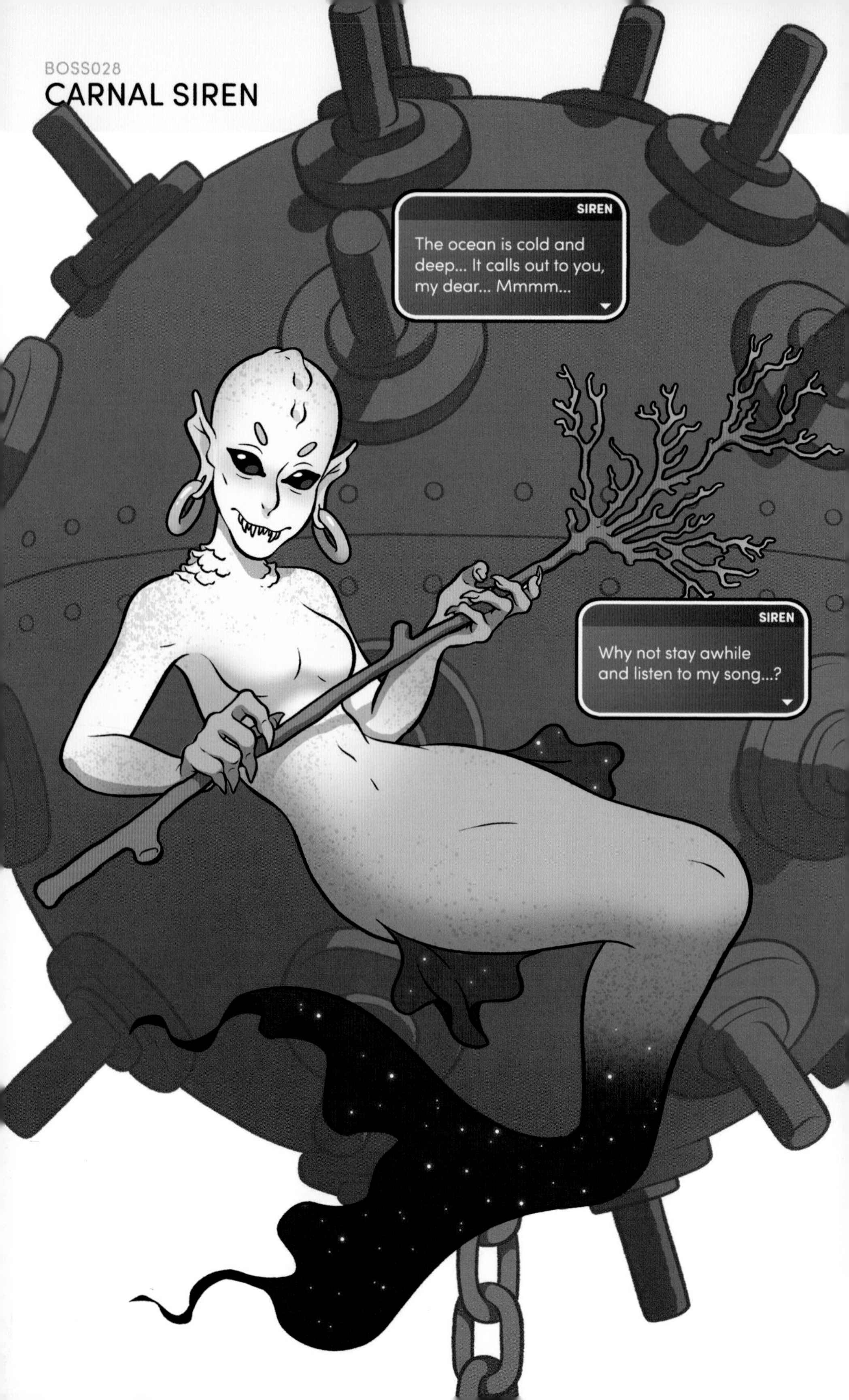
SIREN
The ocean is cold and deep... It calls out to you, my dear... Mmmm...
SIREN
Why not stay awhile and listen to my song...?

SIREN TYPE: ???

Hundreds of years ago, a dreadful pirate queen sailed the open seas. Her impressive fortune was only outmatched by the sheer number of broken hearts she left at ports around the world. One foggy night, her ship arrived at harbor, with only one traumatized sailor aboard. He spoke of his captain being lulled into a trance by a strange and otherwordly song. She became hysterical, murdered nearly her entire crew, and leapt off the ship, never to be seen again. Nobody knows for sure what happened that night, but eerie lullabies can sometimes be heard on moonless nights when the seas are calm...

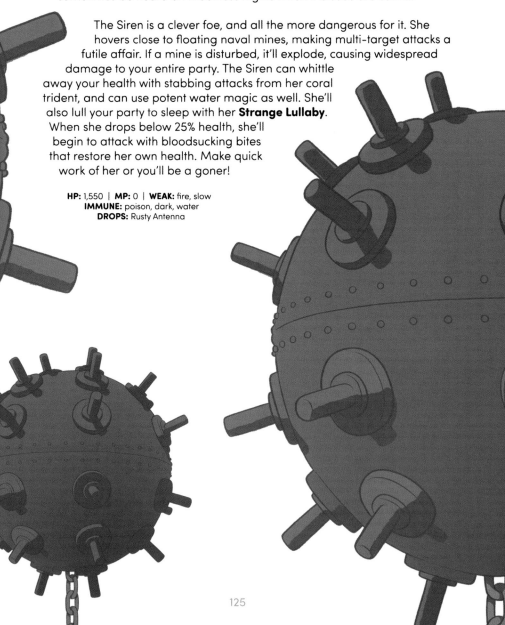

The Siren is a clever foe, and all the more dangerous for it. She hovers close to floating naval mines, making multi-target attacks a futile affair. If a mine is disturbed, it'll explode, causing widespread damage to your entire party. The Siren can whittle away your health with stabbing attacks from her coral trident, and can use potent water magic as well. She'll also lull your party to sleep with her **Strange Lullaby**. When she drops below 25% health, she'll begin to attack with bloodsucking bites that restore her own health. Make quick work of her or you'll be a goner!

HP: 1,550 | **MP:** 0 | **WEAK:** fire, slow
IMMUNE: poison, dark, water
DROPS: Rusty Antenna

CORAL ACCESSORIES

If you collected enough **raw coral** while you were under water, Eddy can use it to craft some useful new accessories to help you on your adventure! Coral accessories vary in what benefits they offer, but all of them **absorb 100% of fire damage**, negating it entirely.

CORAL PENDANT INFO

A simple pendant used for divination purposes. When equipped, enemy stats and weaknesses will be displayed overhead.

CORAL BANGLE INFO

A thick, stylish bangle! Gives a decent boost to physical and magical defense, while also shortening the duration of status ailments.

WORRY STONE INFO

A smooth, oval stone with a thumb-sized indentation. When equipped, the user is immune to **silence** and **dark**.

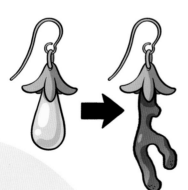

CORAL EARRING INFO

Only available if you retrieved the **Lost Earring** from the carnival grounds at the Pink Witch Circus. A significant upgrade, this new earring gives even greater defense against magical attacks, and like the other coral accessories, negates all fire spells used against the party member.

RUSTY ANTENNA
INFO

A crusty metal antenna with a briny patina, buried in the sea floor and uncovered during the battle with the Siren. It somehow still works! Bring it to Freja, and she might figure out some use for it.

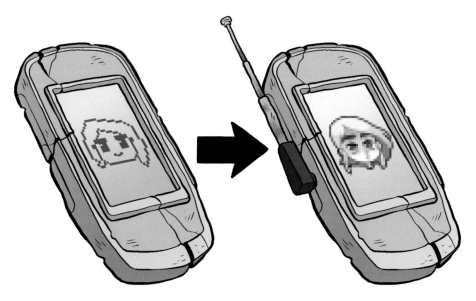

ITEM094
SPRITE 2.0
INFO

By attaching the antenna to the SPRITE system, Freja is able to download a software update! In addition to a cosmetic upgrade, it comes with a few new perks. You can now place delivery orders for certain basic items, like gummies. Also, Claudette can now broadcast her songs across the whole island, boosting team morale and **increasing all EXP** you gain in battle by a cool 10%! A permanent buff! Nice!

Freja needs some time to scan the island, but hopefully she'll be able to pinpoint the location of the evil energy so you can finally get to the bottom of things, once and for all.

If you've helped out every cat you've seen by giving it treats, **Flax** will appear with a letter for you. He came all the way from Harbor City to deliver it to you, so it must be important! It reads as follows:

*"You are cordially invited to **Popoki Hollow**! The queen awaits your arrival. Find the entrance in a tree stump in Thistledew Grasslands. Hurry!"*

SECRET TOWN

INFO

Popoki Hollow is a strange village that seems to exist somewhere in the folds of our own reality. Populated by cats and other small creatures, it's normally a peaceful village, offering refuge to animals who are lost or forgotten, or perhaps just need some respite from humans. You've been invited to visit by the matriarch of the village, but there's one small problem: the entrance is in a seemingly ordinary tree stump out in the Thistledew Grasslands, but only animals can pass through. Since you can't enter in your human state, it seems a little transmogrification is in order! If Esther has learned the **frog** spell, she can transform your party in a jiffy. Otherwise, you'll have to find an enemy who will cast the spell on you. In either case, once you've taken on a froggy form, you can hop through the portal to Popoki Hollow!

Finn

Popoki Hollow is only accessible to animals, so you'll have to stay in frog form the entire time, meaning your strength, defense, and magic will be much weaker. If you transform back into humans, you'll be booted back to the real world, so don't even try it!!!

Penelope

Claudette

Esther

Knox

Theodore

QUEEN ROSEMARY

INFO

Queen Rosemary is the kindly leader of Popoki Hollow. She once belonged to a nice old lady in Harbor City before coming to reside in this mystical forest grove. Life is usually peaceful here, but trouble has found its way to her kingdom. Her most faithful knight has gone missing in **Sludgemire Swamp**, and Rosemary is worried sick. If you can investigate on her behalf, she'll certainly reward you in kind.

KENZO THE BLACKSMITH

INFO

A somewhat gruff but mostly friendly Devon rex whose smithing skills are unmatched in all of Popoki Hollow (which, granted, isn't very large). He'll craft you some new gear, which you'll definitely need!

LEVEL 5 WEAPONS

LUCKY SLUGGER   FINN

A heavy bat with a lucky cat carved into it. Not much of a physical upgrade, but its critical hit percentage is very high.

ATK: 50 | **MAG:** 15 | **CRIT:** 50% | **ELEMENT:** none

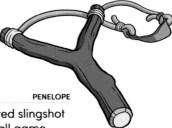

SLINGSHOT   PENELOPE

A simple but finely crafted slingshot used for hunting small game.

ATK: 40 | **MAG:** 60 | **CRIT:** 25% | **ELEMENT:** wind

OLD TAPE   CLAUDETTE

An old, mangled cassette. It once belonged to an eccentric researcher who recorded some odd sounds being transmitted from deep space. How did it end up here...?

ATK: 47 | **MAG:** 75 | **CRIT:** 20% | **ELEMENT:** dark

GOLD BELL   THEODORE

An elegant chime that summons a wildcat to appear and claw an enemy.

ATK: 39 | **MAG:** 70 | **CRIT:** 25% | **ELEMENT:** none

CAT MAGIC   ESTHER

A tiny, pawbound book that belonged to a petite feline wizard. Doesn't contain many spells, but they're quite powerful!

ATK: 0 | **MAG:** 99 | **CRIT:** n/a | **ELEMENT:** n/a

BIG LOG   KNOX

Big log.

ATK: 110 | **MAG:** 0 | **CRIT:** 15% | **ELEMENT:** none

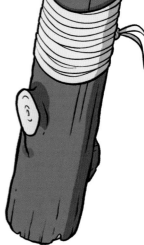

SLUDGEMIRE SWAMP.

DUNGEON

Deeper in Popoki Hollow, beyond the village, there's a bubbling, toxic swamp full of fearsome creatures. Hollow denizens know to keep their distance if they don't want to lose a paw, but it's becoming more difficult as of late. The swamp appears to be expanding, and at an alarming pace. At this rate, it will swallow up Popoki Hollow in a matter of weeks! Queen Rosemary sent her most intrepid knight to investigate, but she never reported back. Find out what became of her and put a stop the the swamp's encroaching expanse! Enemies in the swamp are very weak, but keep in mind that **you are a frog**, so you'll do a fraction of the damage you'd normally do!

EN059A-059B

SWAMP ENEMIES

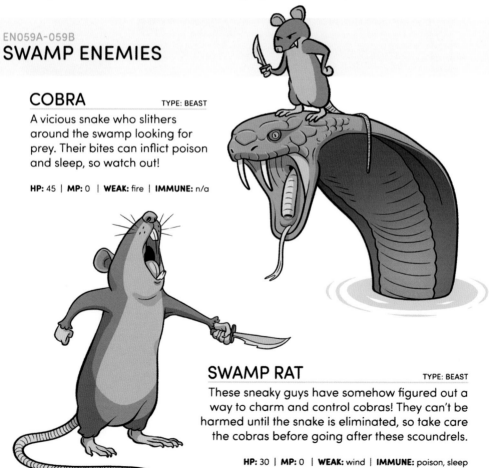

COBRA TYPE: BEAST

A vicious snake who slithers around the swamp looking for prey. Their bites can inflict poison and sleep, so watch out!

HP: 45 | MP: 0 | WEAK: fire | IMMUNE: n/a

SWAMP RAT TYPE: BEAST

These sneaky guys have somehow figured out a way to charm and control cobras! They can't be harmed until the snake is eliminated, so take care the cobras before going after these scoundrels.

HP: 30 | MP: 0 | WEAK: wind | IMMUNE: poison, sleep

SWAMP ENEMIES

SLIMECHILD
TYPE: SLIME

Vicious little soldiers who are fiercely protective of the swamp, snatching any intruders who venture too close and drowning them in the muck. They're covered in a thick coating of mud and slime, which acts as armor, making it hard to defeat them with physical attacks. Either use magic or blast them with water to reveal their true form.

HP: 50 | **MP:** 0 | **WEAK:** water | **IMMUNE:** fire, poison

SPICE KID
TYPE: PLANT

A somewhat weaker version of the Slimechild but still just as mean! They use a spicy breath attack that can induce **frenzy** in your party, but their standard attacks are fairly straightforward.

HP: 50 | **MP:** 0 | **WEAK:** slow | **IMMUNE:** n/a

BOSS029
MEGAFLORA

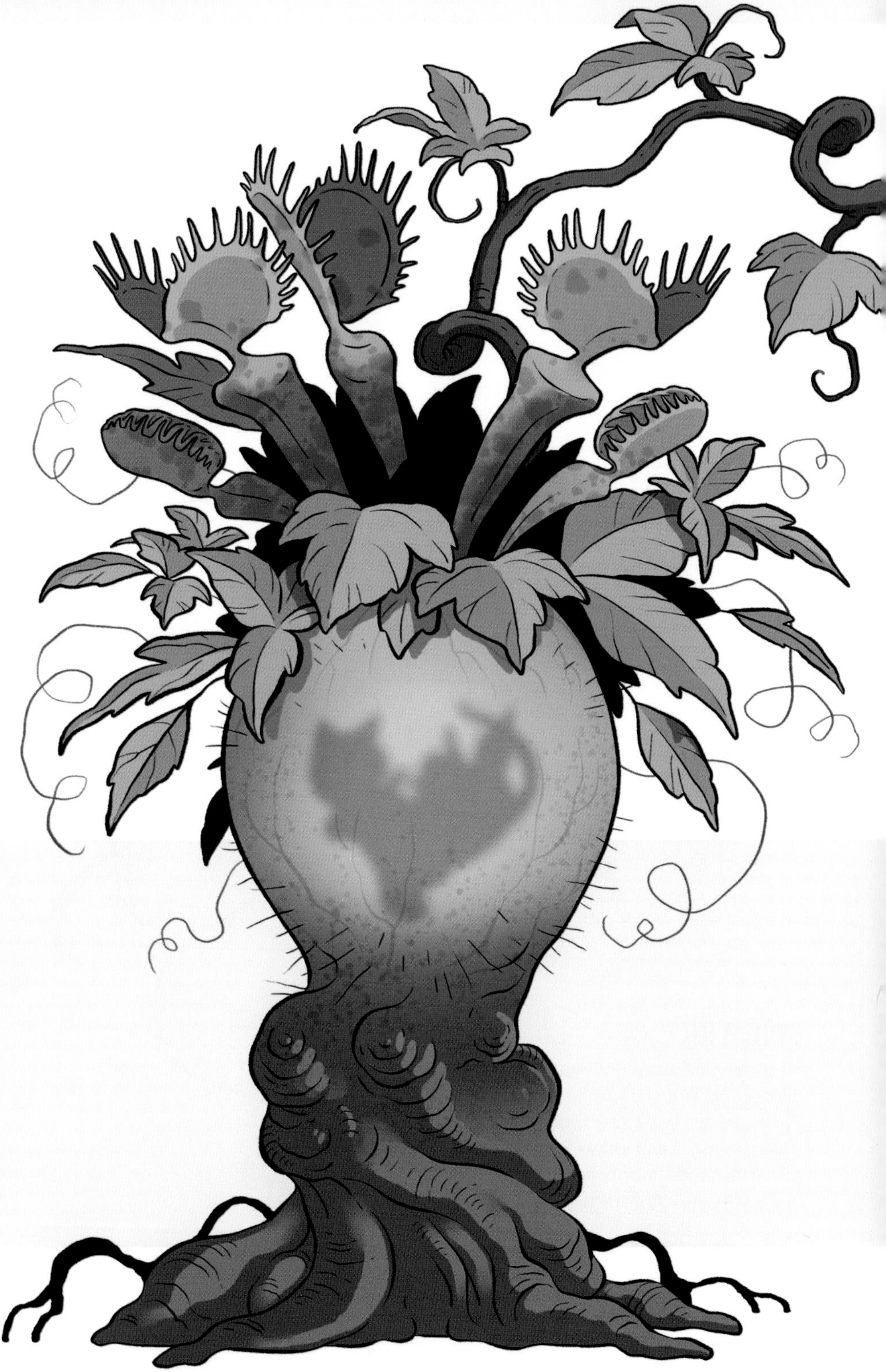

MEGAFLORA

TYPE: PLANT

At the center of Sludgemire Swamp, there's a ravenous carnivorous plant that seems to be growing larger by the day. It slurps up any living thing it can reach, slowly digests it, and uses the energy to pump more toxic sludge into the swamp through its tangled root system. This seems to be what's causing the swamp to expand at such a frightening rate. Thankfully, it appears it just ate something, so it won't gobble you up—though it appears whoever it just consumed is still alive! Be sure to not use any spells that attack multiple targets, or you'll kill whoever is trapped inside!

HP: 200 per head | **MP:** 40 | **WEAK:** fire, slow | **IMMUNE:** poison | **DROPS:** Bea

STATS

WEAPON: BELLSPEAR

STRENGTH

DEFENSE

MAGIC

SPEED

GUTS

LUCK

AFFINITIES

FIRE	WATER	LIGHTNING	WIND	DEBUFFS	SHADOW	LIGHT
B+	F	B	B	B+	B-	B+

BIO

Bea is Queen Rosemary's most intrepid knight (even though she managed to get swallowed up whole by the Megaflora, but that's neither here nor there!). As a reward for stopping the encroaching swamp, Rosemary allows you to enlist Bea's aid on your journey.

Bea is a jack of all trades and can easily fill any gaps you have in your party. You can use a turn to flip her **bellspear**, swapping between physical and magic attacks at will. The magical gold bell can launch powerful spells at enemies, and her spear is sharp enough to lance any foe.

LIKES: sardine snacks, napping, biting people who are being perfectly nice to her

DISLIKES: being wet

In addition to Bea joining your crew, Rosemary allows you to choose one **treasure** from her kingdom to take with you.

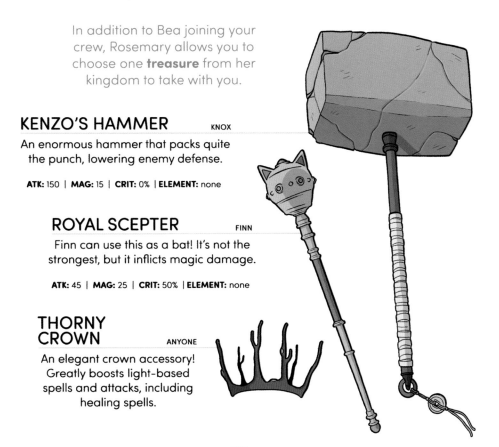

KENZO'S HAMMER   KNOX

An enormous hammer that packs quite the punch, lowering enemy defense.

ATK: 150 | **MAG:** 15 | **CRIT:** 0% | **ELEMENT:** none

ROYAL SCEPTER   FINN

Finn can use this as a bat! It's not the strongest, but it inflicts magic damage.

ATK: 45 | **MAG:** 25 | **CRIT:** 50% | **ELEMENT:** none

THORNY CROWN   ANYONE

An elegant crown accessory! Greatly boosts light-based spells and attacks, including healing spells.

I'm detecting powerful energy on a high peak in the **Cobblerock Mountains**, unlike anything you've encountered before...

GOVERNESS

TYPE: MECHANICAL

An unusual floating robot that appears both ancient and technically advanced at the same time. It makes odd buzzing noises and its exposed wires spark dangerously as it hovers in place. Is this what's been terrorizing the island, causing animals and people to change? What exactly is powering this freakish contraption, and where did it come from? Is this the final boss...?

In battle, the Governess attacks with brutal shocks that can easily lay waste to your party if you're not adequately prepared. Water-based attacks can occasionally cause it to short-circuit, slowing it down temporarily. Make sure you've equipped your strongest weapons and accessories, and pray for a little luck; you might make it through the battle in one piece!

HP: 35,000 | **MP:** 0 | **WEAK:** occasionally water | **IMMUNE:** shadow, lightning | **DROPS:** Fried Hard Drive

GOVERNESS

It appears we've encountered a most unexpected error...

GOVERNESS

FRIED HARD DRIVE

ITEM095

INFO

A hard drive pulled from the remains of the Governess, crafted from some unknown type of stone. It's still warm to the touch, but the data stored inside is corrupted and in a language you'd never understand. Still, it might be of some use to Freja...

Freja is remembering something...

Though the data on the hard drive is corrupted, Freja is able to gather enough information to fill in the blanks of her memory. Here is what she remembers...

Freja's home planet of **Pangella** was a green and prosperous world until it was attacked by a being known as **The Endless**. Perhaps it once had a physical form, but The Endless long ago discovered how to fold itself into the fabric of spacetime, essentially becoming immortal. Left with no material form, it travels the cosmos at will, observing other worlds at its leisure.

Why The Endless chose to attack Freja's world remains a mystery, but she and her companions fought valiantly against the **powerful automatons** The Endless created out of thin air to do its bidding. Freja's companions fell one by one until she was the only survivor, taken prisoner and bound with unbreakable chains, and her mighty golden spear locked away. Fearing that the total destruction of her people was imminent, Freja barely managed to escape, retrieve her spear, and gather every ounce of power she had left. In a desperate final attempt to save her world, Freja used all her energy to open a wormhole, pulling both herself and The Endless into it, not knowing where it would lead or if she'd ever see Pangella again.

That portal opened a million light-years away, over **Starfish Beach**—in fact, directly over an unsuspecting Finneus, swimming out to sea on his surfboard in the early morning dawn. Blinded by the flash of light overhead, Finn hardly noticed an unconscious Freja plummeting to Earth above him...and he barely felt her golden spear slice cleanly through his arm before everything went black...

The Endless has been slowly gaining power by sowing chaos on the island, feeding on people's fear and hatred, and revelling in the violence. Freja knows that this final battle could destroy the island—and perhaps the world—but she has a plan. She reopens the portal at the beach... When you're ready, she can pull both you and The Endless into it, hurtling you all into the past to a time when The Endless wasn't as strong. She has no idea where or when the portal will lead, but hopefully you'll be able to destroy The Endless for good.

Are you ready?

RUINED PLANET LILIUM

DUNGEON INFO

Lilium is a distant planet, totally destroyed by The Endless hundreds of years ago. Crumbling cityscapes dot the horizon, and it's nearly devoid of life. Only the scrappiest vegetation still remains, sprouting defiantly out of the cracked earth, and violent winds blow dust in all directions. The Endless is weaker here with so little life to leech from, but even here its power is profound. This is where the final standoff will take place...

NPC017

ALIEN MERCHANT

??? INFO

This odd creature seems surprised to see you but doesn't appear to be aggressive. It makes some strange noises that you can't decipher, but eventually you infer that it has **wares** to sell you if you so desire. Make sure to stock up on whatever you need before venturing out into the scorched landscape.

Once you've made your purchases, the creature points into the distance at a tall, metallic spire that seems totally out of place in this desolate world. Is this where The Endless will be found?

LEVEL 6 WEAPONS

GLOWSTICK
FINN

A sturdy electric club that serves devastating shock damage to enemies.

ATK: 99 | **MAG:** 19 | **CRIT:** 75%
ELEMENT: non-elemental electric

PHASER
PENELOPE

A laser gun that can be charged up to three times, increasing damage at the cost of regular turns.

ATK: 40/80/120 | **MAG:** 60 | **CRIT:** 0% | **ELEMENT:** n/a

MUSIC BOX
CLAUDETTE

A simple music box that belonged to a young princess, left behind during a great catastrophe. Rotate the crank to bestow various buffs to your party, or play it backward to cause various status ailments to enemies.

ATK: 60 | **MAG:** 110 | **CRIT:** 20% | **ELEMENT:** n/a

STONE FLUTE
THEODORE

A cracked stone recorder that summons a tiny flying saucer to pelt the enemy with radioactive beams of light.

ATK: 55 | **MAG:** 99 | **CRIT:** 35%
ELEMENT: none

OLD TABLET
ESTHER

An ancient stone tablet inscribed with the knowledge of the cosmos. Contains incredibly powerful cosmic spells.

ATK: 0 | **MAG:** 160 | **CRIT:** n/a
ELEMENT: n/a

SNOWCRUSHER
KNOX

A huge sledgehammer that causes mini snowstorms upon impact, occasionally freezing enemies in place.

ATK: 250 | **MAG:** 0 | **CRIT:** 0% | **ELEMENT:** ice

DEATHSPIRE

DUNGEON INFO

An imposing metallic pillar in the middle of a barren wasteland, the Deathspire was created out of nothingness by The Endless as a final form of defense. Smooth and windowless, it appears to glow in the blistering sun. You'll have to climb to the very top to challenge your foe, and there's no telling what dangers await you inside. With no defined form, The Endless can draw on your **fears** to manifest as almost anything, and depending on what it appears as, certain party members may become terrified and have their stats penalized. **Claudette** is the only party member immune to fear, so it's a good idea to keep her in your group!

FINN'S NIGHTMARE TYPE: ORGANIC

The Godhand is an enormous stone arm adorned with mystical rings that offer protection as well as bestowing the boss with a wide range of magic spells. It can use every elemental spell in the game, although each ring can be destroyed, limiting the Godhand to just physical attacks. It's a good idea to destroy the pink kunzite ring first, as it can cast healing spells and buff the boss. However, if you save the pink ring for last while destroying the rings in the order of which they appear in a rainbow, the boss will drop the valuable **Rainbow Ring**. It'll make for a tougher fight, but it might be worth it! While fighting this boss, Finn will be struck with fear, lowering all his stats slightly, so make sure to keep his HP up and consider casting some nice status boosts on him.

ITEM096
RAINBOW RING INFO

A slender ring adorned with a stone that seems to change color depending on how the light hits it. When equipped, it absorbs 50% of the damage dealt by all elemental spells.

GODHAND

KUNZITE INFO
HP: 6,000 | **MP:** 999
WEAK: physical
IMMUNE: silence

PERIDOT INFO
HP: 4,500 | **MP:** 999
WEAK: lightning
IMMUNE: silence

RUBY INFO
HP: 5,000 | **MP:** 999
WEAK: water, ice
IMMUNE: silence

TOPAZ INFO
HP: 5,000 | **MP:** 999
WEAK: wind
IMMUNE: silence

KYANITE INFO
HP: 4,000 | **MP:** 999
WEAK: fire
IMMUNE: silence

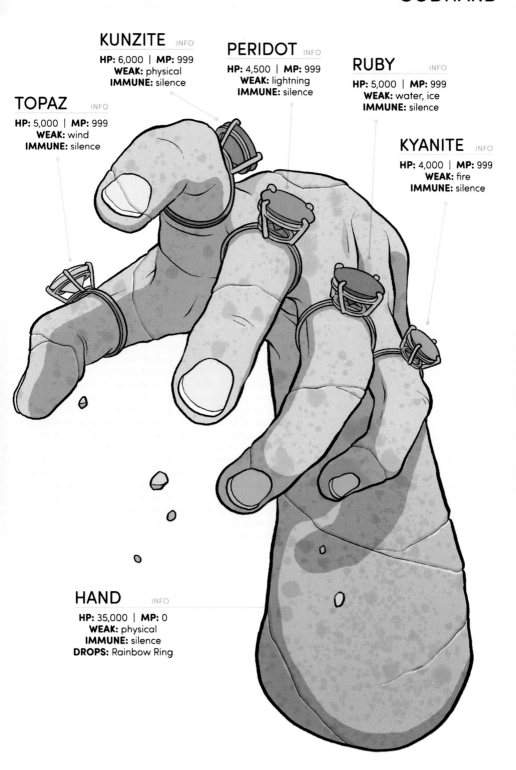

HAND INFO
HP: 35,000 | **MP:** 0
WEAK: physical
IMMUNE: silence
DROPS: Rainbow Ring

PENELOPE'S NIGHTMARE

GIANT CENTIPEDE

TYPE: HUMAN/BUG

An enormous fleshy centipede that scuttles along the walls of the Deathspire, unleashing screams that sound strangely human. When clinging to walls, it can't be reached unless by magic, projectiles, or Penelope's weapons, though she'll be struck by fear during the battle and her accuracy will be lower than usual. The centipede can spew toxin at you, inducing poison. It can also grab you with its many legs, then latch onto you with its gnashing jaws and siphon off HP, restoring itself in the process.

HP: 39,000 | **MP:** 0 | **WEAK:** slow | **IMMUNE:** poison, dark

ESTHER'S NIGHTMARE

PIGARU
TYPE: BEAST

It's everyone's favorite loveable pig character, star of the global media franchise that includes toys, clothing, games, books, cartoons, twenty-four direct-to-video films, and various other product lines and media productions! Last holiday season there was a huge stampede to buy the new talking Pigaru plush; it left seventeen people dead and another eighty gravely injured or permanently maimed. Pigaru's parent company is on track to make $35 billion next year. Isn't that neat?

HP: 45,000 | **MP:** 0 | **WEAK:** fire | **IMMUNE:** dark | **DROPS:** Plastic Ribbon

ITEM097
PLASTIC RIBBON
INFO

A cute little barrette coughed up by Pigaru before dying. Negates all status effects cast upon the wearer.

KNOX'S NIGHTMARE

BRAINCHILD
TYPE: HYBRID

Brainchild is a glistening, floating brain that contains all the most horrible truths of the universe and threatens to bestow knowledge upon you that would drive you mad. It uses extremely powerful dark magic spells, although each eyeball can be individually destroyed to progressively lower the potency of its attacks. Alternatively, if you don't want to focus your time eliminating the eyes, Claudette can cast **dark**, causing them to close temporarily. During this fight, Knox will be struck with fear, making him even weaker to magic than normal. Gulp!

HP: 30,000 | **MP:** 999 | **WEAK:** holy
IMMUNE: silence | **DROPS:** Petrified Eyeball

EYE
INFO

HP: 3,500 | **MP:** 999
WEAK: blind
IMMUNE: silence

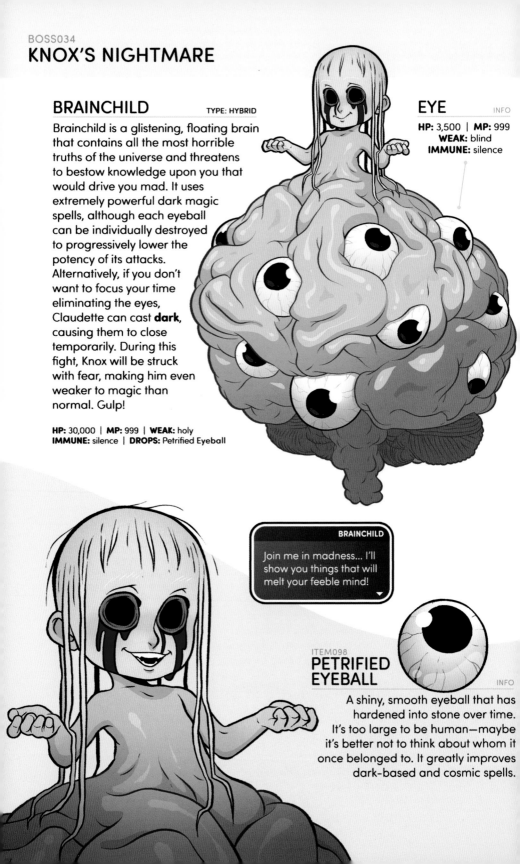

> **BRAINCHILD**
>
> Join me in madness... I'll show you things that will melt your feeble mind!

ITEM098
PETRIFIED EYEBALL
INFO

A shiny, smooth eyeball that has hardened into stone over time. It's too large to be human—maybe it's better not to think about whom it once belonged to. It greatly improves dark-based and cosmic spells.

THEODORE'S NIGHTMARE

RUBY

TYPE: UNDEAD

What's become of poor Ruby?! Well, nothing—
but this grisly illusion of an undead Ruby is a
terrifying sight to behold! Theodore knows it isn't
real, but it's still more than enough to strike fear
in his heart and lower his defense a bit. This
ghastly phantasm uses a variety of status effects
on your party, including **poison, silence, dark,
sleep,** and **curse**. Make sure you have decent
items equipped and be ready to cure your party
in a jiffy. Ruby isn't terribly strong, but your
group can quickly perish if they're afflicted with
too many different maladies at once.

HP: 33,000 | **MP:** 550 | **WEAK:** healing, light
IMMUNE: all status ailments

RUBY

Theeeoooooo..................
.......It's.............soooo......
................coooold............

BOSS036

THE ENDLESS

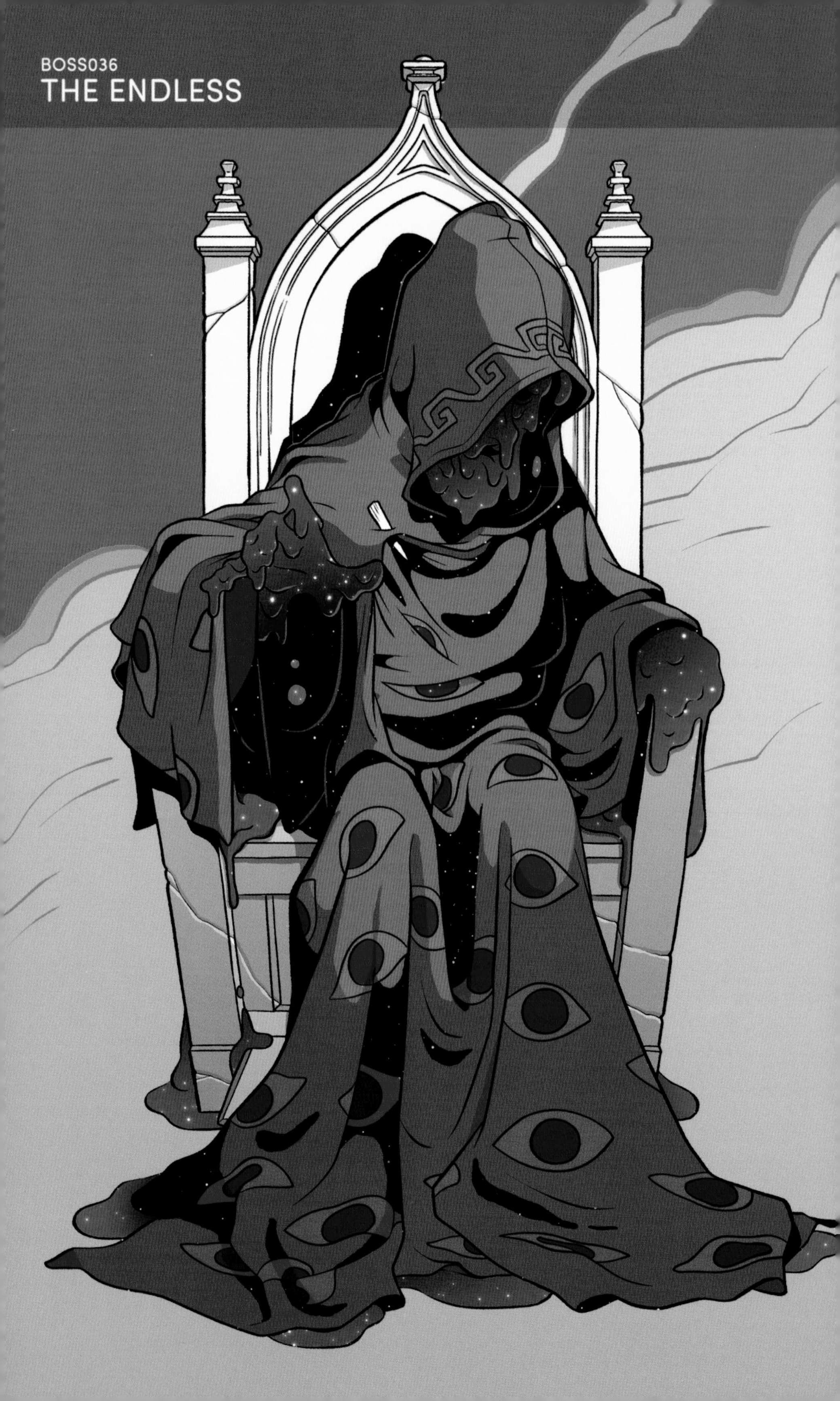

THE ENDLESS

The Endless is an ancient being of mysterious origins. It's unknown if there are others like it, or if it is the only one. For millions of years, it has observed life unfolding on different planets, embedding itself into worlds with advanced life forms, planting the seeds of war and famine, and feeding off the ensuing pain and suffering. It would watch as those civilizations destroyed themselves and then it would abandon the planet to chaos, each cycle making it stronger than before. This is what The Endless did to Freja's home planet of Pangella, and what it will do to Earth if you don't destroy it.

With its various forms defeated as you've climbed the tower, The Endless is in a weakened state—though still deadly. With nothing left to transform into, it tries to morph back into its original physical form, though it's long forgotten what it used to be. What's left is an undulating mass of primordial goo, desperately attempting to morph into something terrifying but failing to solidify. Fearing for its existence, it will use everything in its arsenal to defend itself.

The Endless wields all the strongest elemental spells along with debilitating cosmic magic—including a spell called Ruin, which can instantly fell a single party member, so be ready to revive anyone who gets hit. The Endless has high health and no weakness, but if you have faith and hold tight, you just might prevail...

HP: 99,999 | **MP:** 999 | **WEAK:** n/a | **IMMUNE:** dark, silence, curse, frenzy, sleep

The Endless is defeated and the Deathspire begins to crumble under your feet. With her powers restored, Freja whisks you away, transporting you back to Earth, where everything appears to be returning to normal. The people of Toro Island seem to be coming to their senses, as if waking up from a nightmare. It's almost like nothing happened at all...

On the beach, Freja says goodbye, hoping that the damage done to her homeworld isn't permanent and she can rebuild. She thanks you for your help, then opens a new portal and disappears before your very eyes.

And so, your journey is over.

But is The Endless really gone for good?

If order has been restored to the universe, why do you feel so uneasy...?

CRISIS HAS BEEN
AVERTED...

...THIS TIME.

THANK YOU
FOR PLAYING!

THE END

SIX
MONTHS
LATER...

Finn has received a
postcard from Theo!

Press ❌ to flip over

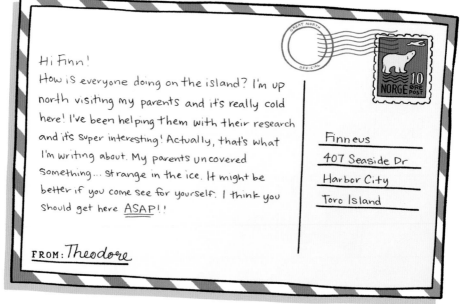

Hi Finn!

How is everyone doing on the island? I'm up north visiting my parents and it's really cold here! I've been helping them with their research and it's super interesting! Actually, that's what I'm writing about. My parents uncovered something... strange in the ice. It might be better if you come see for yourself. I think you should get here <u>ASAP</u>!!

FROM: *Theodore*

Finneus
407 Seaside Dr
Harbor City
Toro Island

NORGE 10 ØRE POST

Andrews McMeel Publishing
a division of Andrews McMeel Universal
1130 Walnut Street, Kansas City, Missouri 64106

www.andrewsmcmeel.com

www.instagram.com/feverknights

22 23 24 25 26 SDB 10 9 8 7 6 5 4 3 2 1

ISBN: 978-1-5248-6286-2

Library of Congress Control Number: 2021945515

Editor: Allison Adler
Art Director: Spencer Williams
Production Editor: Elizabeth A. Garcia
Production Manager: Carol Coe

ATTENTION: SCHOOLS AND BUSINESSES
Andrews McMeel books are available at quantity discounts with bulk purchase for educational, business, or sales promotional use. For information, please e-mail the Andrews McMeel Publishing Special Sales Department: specialsales@amuniversal.com.